The Third Reich: A Layman's Guide

The Third Reich: A Layman's Guide

The Third Reich: A Layman's Guide

Scott Addington

©Scott Addington 2014

All rights reserved

ISBN-10: 1501083333
ISBN-13: 978-1501083334

Other books by Scott Addington:

WW1: A Layman's Guide

WW2: A Layman's Guide

D-Day: A Layman's Guide

Waterloo: A Layman's Guide

The First World War Fact Book

Heroes of The Line

The Great War 100: The First World War in Infographics

Five Minute History: First World War Battles

Five Minute History: First World War Weapons

Heroes of World War 1

All books are available from Amazon sites worldwide

Book cover by Battlefield Design

The right of Scott Addington to be identified as the author of this work has been asserted by him in accordance with the Copyright, Designs and Patents Act 1988.

All rights reserved. No part of this publication may be reproduced, stored in retrieval system, or transmitted, in any form or by any means, electronic, mechanical, photocopying, recording or otherwise, without the prior permission of the copyright owner.

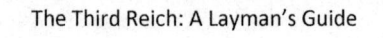

Introduction

Twelve years.

That's all the Third Reich lasted, but despite being relatively short lived, the reverberations of the cruel oppression, the blatant abuse of power, the manipulation of a generation, the earth shattering war and the evil genocide can still be felt today in the twenty-first century. Indeed it feels like entire rainforests have been sacrificed to enable historians of all makes and models to have their two-penneth on the who/why/what/when of this little slice of history that is so nasty, so bemusing and so compelling all at the same time.

How did a seemingly anonymous Austrian born army corporal who, apart from winning the Iron Cross First Class during the First World War hadn't really done anything of note with his life, end up not just gaining the top seat in Germany, but was able to exert such control over his subjects that they would willingly follow him anywhere, even to the brink of self-destruction? Indeed, was he actually as popular as he would like to make out? Was he a powerful and strong dictator or just an emotional wreck that made decisions on a whim with little rhyme or reason? How did a seemingly intelligent and sane population allow themselves to be brainwashed into believing they were building a better brighter future for their children through the annihilation of millions of innocent people?

There are many, many questions…

Following in the style of the other Layman's Guides' this is a relatively short narrative that is more like a chat over a cup of tea rather than a heavy historical text. I have tried to make the story flow naturally albeit without mountains of detail. The chapters here are purposefully written to be short, sharp and to the point, perfect for dipping in and out of whenever the fancy takes you.

The period of the Third Reich is complicated, emotional and often dumbfounding, although my natural style of writing is a little more conversational and relaxed than others, I hope this book comes across as being respectful in its tone, helps readers understand the why/where/when/how/who of the period and inspires further reading across this incredibly important part of European history.

SMA
August 2014

'Those who do not learn from history are doomed to repeat it.'

George Santayana (1863-1952)

Contents

Germany in 1918: The trauma of defeat

Domestic unrest and the struggle of the Weimar Republic

Money, money, money: Hyperinflation

Early anti-Semitism

The Future Fűhrer: DAP Member 555

Hate, hate and more hate: The Nazi manifesto

A war hero and an angry Austrian: Munich 1923

Not exactly Alcatraz: High treason and prison

Dancing on a volcano: The Wall Street Crash

A Republic in Crisis: Elections 1932

Propaganda: The Nazi Political Machine

Power at last: Hitler becomes Chancellor

Chaos and compliance: Towards a one party state

Fire at the Reichstag

Gleichschaltung: The Enabling Act

Gotcha! The Night of the Long Knives

Der Fűhrer

A cultural revolution

The road towards racial paradise

Economic transformation or a cunning ruse?

1935: Dismantling Versailles

The Rhineland

1938: Pressing the pedal to the metal

Anschluss: March 1938

Abandoned and alone: Czechoslovakia

Kristallnacht

An angry Fűhrer and the Pact of Steel

Best Friends Forever (sort of): Germany and Russia

War

Blitzkrieg and initial victories

Genocide

The turning of the tide: 1942-1943

White roses and bomb plots: Germany starts to turn

Liberation and disintegration: 1944-45

The Third Reich on trial: Nuremberg

Germany in 1918: The trauma of defeat

11 November 1918. It is, without doubt, one of the most famous dates in modern European history. At 11am on that historic day, the German High Command surrendered to the Allies and signed the Armistice that brought to an end the First World War.

At this time Germany was in a mess. Sailors had mutinied in the ports of Hamburg, Kiel and Wilhelmshaven; old soldiers had set up revolutionary councils in Berlin and other cities across the country; the general population was hurting due to the Allied blockade that forced rations to be reduced to minuscule levels. Eventually the German Emperor, Kaiser Wilhelm II, fled to Holland and was replaced by a democratic government whose first act was to negotiate peace. For many millions of Germans the end of the war was a long awaited relief.

It was a bit different at the front line, however. To many of the German soldiers in the trenches the news of the surrender and Armistice came out of nowhere; they were still occupying huge swathes of enemy territory and certainly didn't feel like they were beaten. Granted 1918 hadn't been the best of years for the army but many were still confident of ultimate victory and many struggled to understand why the surrender had happened in the first place. When the order came to evacuate their positions as quickly as they could there was confusion, anger and bewilderment amongst the men. To them such actions brought only shame and dishonour onto the German Army and as they trudged home senior army leaders were convinced they had been 'stabbed in the back' by an unseen enemy from within Germany itself. They were angry, frustrated and they were looking for scapegoats.

Post war Germany struggled with the concept of peace in the immediate aftermath of the Armistice. It continued to function on a war footing – at war with itself in many respects – in a desperate search to find who was responsible for humiliating the Fatherland.

In early 1919 Germany was a political melting pot on the verge of revolution with fear and hatred ruling the streets. Everyone was blaming everyone else for the demise of their country, and running battles, assassinations, riots, beatings and general civil unrest were daily occurrences.

It was in this melting pot that the Weimar Republic tried to bring order and democracy to Germany.

Domestic unrest and the struggle of the Weimar Republic

After kicking out the Kaiser, Germany chose to go down the route of a democratically elected government for the first time in her history. On 11 February 1919, Friedrich Ebert, the leader of the German Social Democratic Party (SDP), was elected as the first President of the new German Republic. Ebert took control of a Germany that was volatile to say the least. Social unrest had spread like wildfire on the back of the defeat and in the first few months of 1919 Ebert struggled to keep political control in many regions of the country.

In Munich, the capital of Bavaria, there was complete chaos. The local socialist politician, Kurt Eisner, was assassinated in February 1919 and a few months later the 'Räterepublik' – a pseudo Communist regional government – led by a number of Jews – was formed. This council didn't last long however as armed groups such as the Freikorps brutally set about the Communists during 1 and 2 May and snuffed them out. The Freikorps was made up of ex-soldiers with right wing tendencies that were happy to support the government. Even though they disliked the Social Democrats they hated the Communists even more and were delighted to give them (the Communists) a kicking at any opportunity. By mid-1919 there were almost two hundred Freikorps groups across the country and they were all very busy (and very happy) snuffing out any Communist uprising.

Inspired by the 1917 Russian Revolution a number of similar attempted Communist uprisings popped up in various parts of Germany, including a large attempt by the Spartakists (part of the KDP – the German Communist Party) to seize Berlin. The situation in Berlin was so bad that in order to finalise a constitution for Germany, Ebert and the SDP relocated to the more peaceful city of Weimar.

One of first things Ebert and his government had to do was to 'negotiate' (I use the term negotiate in its loosest possible sense) the Treaty of Versailles. The general feeling in Germany was that because the war had finished without the Allies stepping foot into Germany, and because the Kaiser and been shunted into the Netherlands and a democratic government put in his place, the terms of peace wouldn't be overly harsh.

They were to be disappointed.

Germany lost 13% of her territory and with that chunk of land went 10% of her total population. She was also forced to accept total responsibility for the war. As a consequence of this, and to deter Germany from lacing up her gloves again, huge reparations (fines) were ordered to be paid and the German Army was restricted to just 100,000 men. No tanks, big guns or conscription were allowed, and millions of rifles, weapons and military supplies had to be handed over. No new military ships could be built and Germany was not allowed an effective air force. The terms of the Treaty were simply humiliating and if there was a feeling of frustration in Germany beforehand, once the Treaty had been signed that frustration turned to outrage.

As well as the fallout from Versailles, Ebert and the Weimar Republic had other issues to contend with. The growing threat of a Communist uprising forced the Weimar Republic to rely on right wing paramilitary groups to help keep any Communist group in check. Hundreds of these partisan groups sprung up, fueled by thousands of disaffected soldiers that had returned from the war still with their uniform and weapons (their retreat had been so haphazard that there had been no formal disarming of soldiers). These men could not be disarmed nor were they loyal to the government. One such bunch was a group of 'brownshirts' that represented a certain German Workers Party (DAP).

Another big problem for the Weimar Republic was the way it was structured. The voting system in Germany was based on proportional representation, which encouraged the proliferation of numerous small political parties making it hard to form a strong government that could make tough decisions, thus weakening the new democracy.

The middle class was largely biased towards the right wing nationalist groups. They distrusted the Weimar Republic and had little sympathy for their overall idea of a democratic Germany. Similarly, the army, what was left of it, had little time for the new Republic and was not particularly helpful when they were needed to try and calm things down. Again, these things made it very hard to establish a strong and credible democratic government.

If that lot wasn't enough, the Weimar government was struggling to keep a steady hand on the economy. Over the last four and a bit years Germany had lost the thick end of two million men in the war. These were the core of Germany's work force and Germany's industrial base could not recover without them. Add in the French occupation of the German Ruhr industrial area, plus the enormous reparations that the Allies were forcing them to pay as part of the Treaty of Versailles, and it was easy to see that Germany was about to stare down the barrel of an economic crisis.

Money, money, money: Hyperinflation

Now, if the Weimar Republic had managed to deliver a certain amount of economic stability and a decent outlook in terms of jobs to the German population, especially the returning soldiers, they would have had a fighting chance of being a success. Unfortunately, this wasn't to be the case and right from the off the Weimar Republic was hit by rather large financial bombs from all over the place.

Firstly there was the cost of the war itself. After 1916 the cost of war far outstripped any monies that could be raised by taxes, loans and other such means. Throughout the war the Germans were printing money for fun to generate enough cash in the system to feed the war machine, however it was a massive gamble and, ultimately, they lost the bet. The recovery plan too was dependent on victory. With that victory would come the annexation of large industrial land and the receipt of huge piles of cash and gold in the form of Allied reparation payments that would have been sufficient to pay off the German debt. In the end though, ultimate defeat meant that the shoe was on the other foot as Germany herself had to suffer the annexation of some of her own industrial land as well as some heavy financial bills at the hands of the Allies.

That annexation of industrial land by the Allies hit Germany hard. Fertile industrial areas such as Alsace and Lorraine had to be given back to France under the terms of the Treaty of Versailles, and as a result industrial output in 1919 was just 42% of what it had been in 1913 and grain production was half what it was before the war.

The economy was put under further strain by the need to provide help and welfare to the returning soldiers, especially those who were wounded and couldn't work. The natural way for the government to try and pay for all of this would have been to raise taxes, but with the huge amount of civil unrest all across the country, there would have been carnage if they had done this.

The bottom line was that Germany couldn't pay the reparations. They had also fallen significantly behind in payments of coal to France, another clause of Versailles. In an effort to get what they were owed, the French took it upon themselves to march into the leading German industrial area, the Ruhr, and try and take the coal for themselves. The Weimar Republic declared a state of passive resistance and urged everyone in the Ruhr to adopt a stance of non-cooperation with the French. It worked for a while, but in the long run it only made matters worse.

The cumulative effect of all of this financial mismanagement was inflation. Before the war any German citizen wanting to purchase an American dollar would need to stump up four German marks, in July 1923 that same American dollar commanded 353,000 German marks and in December that number rose to an incredible 4,200,000,000,000 German marks. That number is so big I am not sure I know the correct way to say it.

Such hyperinflation made it almost impossible to import any kind of food or supplies from abroad and the threat of starvation for millions of people was very real. Food riots, looting and fights with farmers were commonplace. Businesses and public services such as trams and trains gradually stopped working as they could not afford to pay their workers. Slowly but surely, Germany was grinding to a halt, something needed to be done. Fast.

Enter Gustav Stresemann.

When Stresemann became Foreign Minister in August 1923 he quickly ordered the workers of the Ruhr back to work and then immediately held negotiations with the French that saw them retreat from the Ruhr region in return for a guarantee over reparation payments. In addition, the Allies agreed to re-visit the terms of the reparations and American economist Charles Dawes drew up a revised payment plan that ensured that Germany could at least afford the repayments. The American government also agreed to loan Germany some cash to help them out, which was nice of them.

In an effort to tackle the hyper-inflation issue, Stresemann looked to a chap called Hjalmar Schacht to head up the central bank. A new currency, the rentenmark, was introduced and was linked to the price of gold, eventually this new currency became more widely accepted, its name was changed to the reichmark and it became the new German currency. By the end of 1924 hyper-inflation was over.

The quick and decisive actions of both Stresemann and Schacht stabilised Germany and over the next five years the economy steadily regained its strength. New factories were built, employment improved and things in general began to return to normal.

Wunderbar!

Early anti-Semitism

There had been a degree of anti-Semitism quietly bubbling away in Germany for centuries. It was only since the back-end of the nineteenth century that Jews were able to own land and farm it. Twentieth century Germany wasn't much better and after the war anti-Semitism kicked on to the next level. There were strong rumours that many Jews had managed to avoid war service, and there were other rumours flying around about how a Jewish member of the government (Walther Rathenau) had sneakily orchestrated the humiliating Armistice. On top of this, there were many people who believed in a grand conspiracy theory that Germany was under attack from an organised group of influential Jews that were dedicated to bringing Germany to her knees. This final theory was given significant fuel when it was discovered that many of the leaders of the attempted communist-led coup involving the Munich Rästerepublik were in fact Jewish. This just served to reinforce the prejudice that the Jews were responsible for all that was wrong with post-war Germany.

It was perhaps slightly ironic that there were hardly any Jews living in Germany at that time. In 1933 there were around half a million Jews recorded, that was less than 1% of the population. Not exactly the makings of a religious uprising. Also, most of these Jews had mingled and mixed well into the existing population, unlike their counterparts in other European countries such as Poland.

Interestingly, the lack of numbers helped the Germans spread the negative stories about Jews as there was no one with a voice strong or loud enough to stand up and try to stop them. It was therefore quite easy to conjure up a fantasy (negative) image of the average Jew and of Jewishness. Very quickly the Jews became synonymous with everything that was wrong with post-war Germany. They were blamed for left wing politics; they were blamed for pedalling exploitative capitalism, for degenerate cultural ideas and for the secularisation of the population... You name it, it was their fault.

The façade of the Jewish population wasn't helped by a steady influx of 'eastern Jews' from countries such as Poland and Russia who moved to Germany to get away from persecution in their own country. These 'eastern Jews' struggled to mix and settle properly in their new homeland and their sometimes disruptive behavior did nothing to help the perception of Jewishness in the eyes of the indigenous German population.

It was against this back drop that a 30-year-old German Army corporal wandered into a meeting of the German Workers' Party that was taking place on 12 September 1919 in the Veterans' Hall of the Sterneckerbräu beer hall in Munich. At the meeting the corporal rounded on one of the speakers, a professor Baumann who was championing Bavarian independence from Germany and joining up with

Austria, and completely destroyed his arguments. After a heated exchange, the professor left the hall with his tail well and truly between his legs.

The corporal in question was Adolf Hitler and after watching him in action Anton Drexler, the founder of the DAP, immediately asked him to join. Hitler accepted.

The Future Fűhrer: DAP Member 555

Hitler's early life was nothing special. He was no good at school, he was rejected by the Academy of Graphic Arts in Vienna, he struggled to make friends, he struggled to make money and was viewed by many as being a bit… well, weird.

Indeed the only real achievement in his life before he set foot in the Sterneckerbräu beer hall in Munich that fateful day in September 1919 was him winning the Iron Cross First Class as a Corporal in the German Army. Ironically, his commanding officer who recommended him for this award was Jewish. The First World War finally gave Hitler something to believe in and he remembered it as his 'greatest and most unforgettable time of my earthly existence'. When war broke out in 1914 he immediately tried to enlist in the German Army, but because he was Austrian he was rejected. A quick letter to the authorities swearing his allegiance and devotion to all things German did the trick though and he was soon lining up as a soldier with the 16th Bavarian Reserve Regiment.

Hitler was not your typical soldier. He didn't get drunk and he didn't seek out the special attention of certain working ladies either. He was definitely not 'one of the lads'. He much preferred the company of his sketchbook and a white terrier dog he adopted in the trenches. If he did engage in conversation with any of his fellow soldiers he would more than likely launch into a lengthy monologue on whatever subject he was pondering at that time, often boring his colleagues rigid.

When the war finally finished in November 1918 Hitler was in hospital recovering from the effects of a gas attack. To say he was gutted at the news of the defeat was an understatement and he quickly jumped on the bandwagon that someone, somewhere had 'stabbed Germany in the back' and forced her to surrender.

Hitler was determined to stay in the army if he could to avoid having to return to a dull civilian existence; spells as a border guard in prisoners of war camps followed before he was asked to consider being a political instructor to ensure that the soldiers had not been too influenced by communism. He jumped at the chance and started to monitor the political situation in Munich, reporting back to his superiors on his findings. On 12 September 1919 he was asked to keep an eye on a right wing party that went by the name of the Germany Workers Party (Deutsche Arbeiter Partei: DAP).

During his appearance at this meeting in Munich, Hitler showed a glimpse of his obvious talent for public speaking. The party leader at that time, Anton Drexler, knew at once that someone with Hitler's oratory skills could be very useful. Hitler soon joined up as member number 555; the party started their membership system at the number 500 to make it seem that they were bigger than they actually were.

Hate, hate and more hate: The Nazi manifesto

Within a few months of joining the DAP, Hitler soon began to attract larger and larger crowds to his talks. He was desperate for the party to turn it up a notch and hold mass meetings that could accommodate thousands of people rather than just a few hundred squashed in like sardines, but the senior DAP members were nervous about holding such big events as they were worried they would attract too many communists that would start trouble. Hitler, however, didn't care about that, in fact he welcomed it, thinking it as a potentially good PR stunt to help cement the party's position as being strongly anti-communist.

On 24 February 1920 Hitler's prayers were answered. When he wandered in to deliver his speech on this day in Munich he was greeted by a crowd of two thousand – many of whom were communists hell bent on heckling.

The speech he delivered that evening was historical. Not just because it heralded a new, bigger, bolder era for the DAP, but this was the first time that he presented the party's manifesto. Up until this point the DAP had been a noisy and raucous party, but possessed little political substance. If they were to be taken seriously they needed some definite and tangible policies. Hitler outlined these during his speech in twenty-five separate points.

At first he struggled to make himself heard with the large communist group nosily heckling him, then it all kicked off in the crowd with several large fights breaking out between rival political groups. Eventually Hitler was able to resume his speech, and if his statement in his autobiography 'Mein Kampf' can be believed, the shouting, fighting and heckling were gradually drowned out by applause.

The twenty-five points were a mix of extreme nationalism, a large dose of racism, combined with a pinch or two of socialism:

1. We demand the unification of all Germans in the Greater Germany on the basis of the right of self-determination of peoples.

2. We demand equality of rights for the German people in respect to the other nations; abrogation of the peace treaties of Versailles and St. Germain.

3. We demand land and territory (colonies) for the sustenance of our people, and colonisation for our surplus population.

4. Only a member of the race can be a citizen. A member of the race can only be one who is of German blood, without consideration of creed. Consequently no Jew can be a member of the race.

5. Whoever has no citizenship is to be able to live in Germany only as a guest, and must be under the authority of legislation for foreigners.

6. The right to determine matters concerning administration and law belongs only to the citizen. Therefore we demand that every public office, of any sort whatsoever, whether in the Reich, the county or municipality, be filled only by citizens. We combat the corrupting parliamentary economy, office-holding only according to party inclinations without consideration of character or abilities.

7. We demand that the state be charged first with providing the opportunity for a livelihood and way of life for the citizens. If it is impossible to sustain the total population of the State, then the members of foreign nations (non-citizens) are to be expelled from the Reich.

8. Any further immigration of non-citizens is to be prevented. We demand that all non-Germans, who have immigrated to Germany since 2 August 1914, be forced immediately to leave the Reich.

9. All citizens must have equal rights and obligations.

10. The first obligation of every citizen must be to work both spiritually and physically. The activity of individuals is not to counteract the interests of the universality, but must have its result within the framework of the whole for the benefit of all. Consequently we demand:

11. Abolition of unearned (work and labour) incomes. Breaking of rent-slavery.

12. In consideration of the monstrous sacrifice in property and blood that each war demands of the people personal enrichment through a war must be designated as a crime against the people. Therefore we demand the total confiscation of all war profits.

13. We demand the nationalisation of all (previous) associated industries (trusts).

14. We demand a division of profits of all heavy industries.

15. We demand an expansion on a large scale of old age welfare.

16. We demand the creation of a healthy middle class and its conservation, immediate communalization of the great warehouses and their being leased at low cost to small firms, the utmost consideration of all small firms in contracts with the State, county or municipality.

17. We demand a land reform suitable to our needs, provision of a law for the free expropriation of land for the purposes of public utility, abolition of taxes on land and prevention of all speculation in land.

18. We demand struggle without consideration against those whose activity is injurious to the general interest. Common national criminals, usurers, Schieber and so forth

are to be punished with death, without consideration of confession or race.

19. We demand substitution of a German common law in place of the Roman law serving a materialistic world-order.

20. The state is to be responsible for a fundamental reconstruction of our whole national education programme, to enable every capable and industrious German to obtain higher education and subsequently introduction into leading positions. The plans of instruction of all educational institutions are to conform to the experiences of practical life. The comprehension of the concept of the State must be striven for by the school [Staatsbuergerkunde] as early as the beginning of understanding. We demand the education at the expense of the State of outstanding intellectually gifted children of poor parents without consideration of position or profession.

21. The State is to care for the elevating national health by protecting the mother and child, by outlawing child-labour, by the encouragement of physical fitness, by means of the legal establishment of a gymnastic and sport obligation, by the utmost support of all organisations concerned with the physical instruction of the young.

22. We demand abolition of the mercenary troops and formation of a national army.

23. We demand legal opposition to known lies and their promulgation through the press. In order to enable the

provision of a German press, we demand, that: a. All writers and employees of the newspapers appearing in the German language be members of the race: b. Non-German newspapers be required to have the express permission of the State to be published. They may not be printed in the German language: c. Non-Germans are forbidden by law any financial interest in German publications, or any influence on them, and as punishment for violations the closing of such a publication as well as the immediate expulsion from the Reich of the non-German concerned. Publications which are counter to the general good are to be forbidden. We demand legal prosecution of artistic and literary forms which exert a destructive influence on our national life, and the closure of organizations opposing the above made demands.

24. We demand freedom of religion for all religious denominations within the State so long as they do not endanger its existence or oppose the moral senses of the Germanic race. The Party as such advocates the standpoint of a positive Christianity without binding itself confessionally to any one denomination. It combats the Jewish-materialistic spirit within and around us, and is convinced that a lasting recovery of our nation can only succeed from within on the framework: common utility precedes individual utility.

25. For the execution of all of this we demand the formation of a strong central power in the Reich. Unlimited authority of the central parliament over the whole Reich and its

organisations in general. The forming of state and profession chambers for the execution of the laws made by the Reich within the various states of the confederation. The leaders of the Party promise, if necessary by sacrificing their own lives, to support by the execution of the points set forth above without consideration.

Taken from Document No. 1708-PS of the Nuremburg Trials, (Yale Law School)

Over the next four hours Adolf Hitler laid out the twenty-five points that underpinned the political ethos of the DAP, he went through each point in glorious detail and asked the rowdy crowd for their approval on each one. He got what he wanted, unanimous approval and support.

The meeting was a huge success.

It didn't take long before Hitler's gift for tub-thumping speeches were making a name for both himself and his party, which started to grow in members steadily. Within two years Hitler was talking regularly in front of thousands of people and it was clear that Hitler was the party's main man. He was by far their most valuable and marketable asset, and he knew it. In June 1921 he threatened to resign after Drexler had the temerity to question his leadership. The bluff worked and instead of walking out the door, he was confirmed as party chairman and overall top dog.

The subsequent few years saw the party, especially the paramilitary wing of the party, grow steadily. Violence and intimidation followed them wherever they went and soon the group was banned in almost every German state apart from Bavaria.

One of Hitler's first acts as leader was to change the name of the party so it included the term 'National Socialist'. From now on the party was called the National Socialist German Workers' Party (Nationalsozialistische Deutsche Arbeiterpartei or NSDAP). Or for short, the Nazi Party. Then, realising that his party needed a symbol or flag of identity, Hitler finally decided on a black swastika placed inside a white circle on a red background. Powerful, strong and slightly menacing to boot, it was to become one of the most recognisable and most infamous party symbols or flags in the history of history.

The flag certainly helped with the party's popularity and by the end of 1920 it had about three thousand active members.

Hitler was becoming more and more convinced that only way Germany would get out of the mess she found herself in would be for someone (him) to forcibly overthrow the government and tear up the Treaty of Versailles. In 1923, a few things happened, none of which were directly of Hitler's making, that presenting him an ideal opportunity.

An opportunity for revolution.

A war hero and an angry Austrian: Munich 1923

One of the key members of Hitler's staff in the early 1920s was Ernst Rhöm. He was a career soldier and a violent man who glorified the rough and brutal lifestyle of the Army. He was also a highly regarded and influential staff officer with his fingers in many pies. Rhöm brokered a number of deals that brought a number of armed 'patriotic leagues' together under the name of the Deutscher Kampfbund (The German Fighting Union), putting huge numbers of paramilitary resources at Hitler's disposal.

Meanwhile Germany was once more on the verge of crisis. The passive resistance in the Ruhr had stopped and Germany was again repaying huge reparations. The region of Bavaria was not happy at this and named a right wing politician, Gustav von Kahr, as their head of state, with General Otto von Lossow (commander of the Reichswehr) and Colonel Hans von Seisser (head of state police) as his leadership big-wigs. The three of them now ruled Bavaria and started to make it very publicly known their dislike of the whole situation, especially the French occupation of the Ruhr. To the politicians in Berlin It looked like Bavaria was about to split from Germany. Tensions were high, a state of emergency was declared in Berlin for the whole of the country, but this was ignored in Bavaria.

It was complete chaos but in such disorder Hitler saw an opportunity.

Lossow was readying his army troops for an armed assault on the French in the Ruhr and ordered all of the weapons owned by the various right-wing Bavarian paramilitary groups to be handed over to his men; in return he started to train these paramilitary men as auxiliaries. Hitler was named political leader of these paramilitaries, but German legend and icon, General Ludendorff, was declared the overall figurehead. However Kahr, Lossow and Seisser failed to get the backing of the German Army for their plans. General Hans von Seeckt, the leader of the German Army, preferred to bring down the government quietly by the back door, rather than a full on frontal assault.

The 'revolution' was cancelled. This put Hitler in an awkward position as he had about 3,000 rabid paramilitaries knocking on his door and itching for a fight. It was now or never for Hitler, if he didn't act quickly there was a big danger that these men would turn and desert him. He had to act on his own and force Kahr, Lossow and Seisser to support him.

It was then announced that Kahr would be a keynote speaker at a meeting of local business leaders in Munich's Buergerbraukeller on the outskirts of the city. The date set for the meeting was 8 November 1923. Seisser and Lossow would also be attending. It was an opportunity Hitler could not pass up. He got busy at once organising his paramilitary 'storm troopers'.

It was time to start the revolution.

Kahr took to the stage at about 8.15pm. Way before that Hitler and his supporters began their march towards the Buergerbraukeller. Half an hour into his speech in front of 3,000 local business people, Hitler's storm troopers surrounded the building and even set up a machine gun post at the entrance. Hitler forced his way into the hall, jumped on a table, fired his pistol into the air and shouted 'The national revolution has begun!' He then took his place on the stage in front of the bemused Kahr, where he continued to address the stunned audience: 'This building is occupied by 600 heavily armed men. No one may leave this hall... The Bavarian and Reich governments have been removed and a provisional national government has been formed. The army and the police are marching on the city under the swastika banner.'

The comment about the governments being removed was completely made up of course, but no-one in that hall was in a position to question him. What they did know was that Hitler was real and in their hall making a lot of noise. His pistol was real, as were the storm troopers and their rifles and the machine gun. They all looked on helplessly as Hitler ushered Kahr, Lossow and Seisser into a private room. However, the three Bavarian leaders refused to cooperate, even when a hysterical Hitler threatened to kill everyone, including himself, if they didn't comply with his requests. It was no use though. The putsch was beginning to crumble in front of his eyes.

In an instant, Hitler ran back into the hall and declared that the three leaders in the adjoining room had agreed to join him in forming a new government and that General Ludendorff had agreed to take over the leadership of a new German army. It was a bluff of epic proportions, but it worked beautifully. The crowd erupted into loud cheers. Then Ludendorff himself appeared. Although annoyed that his name had been used without him knowing, he advised the three leaders to cooperate in the interest of Germany. Over-awed by being in the presence of Ludendorff and the reaction of the cheering crowd, all three men agreed and accompanied a delighted Hitler back on the stage where they all made a short speech and swore loyalty to the new regime.

For Hitler, it was all going swimmingly. But it would not last.

News of the coup soon got out to Berlin who ordered the army to suppress any disorder. Hitler decided to march as planned the following morning onto the centre of the city of Munich. With Ludendorff at his side, he was confident that no soldier or policeman would dare to shoot at the legendary commander who had delivered Germany's greatest military victories in both the east and the west. In fact, once they saw him at the head of the column, Hitler was convinced they would drop their weapons and join them in revolution.

At about 11am on 9 November Hitler and Ludendorff led about 3,000 Nazi's out of the Buergerbraukeller towards the city centre. Amongst the marching group were personalities such as Joseph Goebbels, Hermann Göring, Rudolph Hess and Heinrich Himmler. Their main objective was the War Ministry. Röhm and a group of his storm troopers advanced ahead of the marching column but were quickly surrounded by members of the Reichswehr when they approached the War Ministry. As Hitler and Ludendorff approached the scene, shots were fired. The firing only lasted a minute or so but there were many casualties. Sixteen Nazis were killed along with a number of policemen and many more were wounded including Göring and Hitler himself. Everyone in the advancing column had hit the ground to avoid the gunfire. Everyone that is except Ludendorff. He continued to march tall and proud like a proper soldier. But he marched alone. No one followed his soldierly example. Not even Hitler, who was hustled quickly into a car and driven at speed away from the scene. Leaving his dead and dying comrades in the street where they fell.

Not exactly Alcatraz: High treason and prison

Within a matter of days all of the leading personalities of the attempted coup were rounded up and put behind bars. It was over. National Socialism was dead, its leader's fledgling political career over.

Or was it?

When his trial opened, Hitler knew he potentially faced the death penalty for high treason and the deaths of four policemen. This didn't faze him though; instead he saw his trial as a huge opportunity. The world's press would be assembled for his trial and this gave him the opportunity of a public platform for him to raise his profile throughout Germany and beyond.

Although most of the press came to see Ludendorff, Hitler at once grabbed the limelight and proceeded to dominate the courtroom. He was able to pull some strings and call in a few favours from some influential friends, including the Bavarian Minister of Justice, to allow a very lenient courtroom; his opening statement went on for four hours and he was allowed to speak on his own behalf whenever he liked and also to cross examine witnesses.

In summing up his final defence he declared: 'I alone bear the responsibility. But I am not a criminal because of that.

There is no such thing as high treason against the traitors of 1918.'

In the end Ludendorff was acquitted, whilst Hitler and the other Nazis were found guilty. Hitler was sentenced to five years behind bars and hit with a fine of two hundred gold marks. He was then sent to Landsberg prison.

During his imprisonment he enjoyed a large and comfortable cell with many creature comforts. He was allowed as many visitors as he could handle and was also permitted to dictate his autobiography (Mein Kampf) to his two colleagues, Emil Maurice and Rudolf Hess, who were imprisoned with him. It wasn't exactly Alcatraz and five days before Christmas 1924 he was released after serving just nine months.

Adolf Hitler was back in business.

However, when he walked out through the prison gates, he was not exactly welcomed back into political society with open arms and an oompah party. The NSDAP was banned, its former leaders were publically squabbling and he himself was forbidden from speaking in public. Worse still, the Weimar Republic, under the stewardship of Gustav Stresemann, was finally getting to grips with running the country properly and Germany was beginning to enjoy a period of stability and, whisper it quietly, moderate prosperity. Under these more positive conditions the requirement for a noisy, aggressive, anti-establishment party such as the NSDAP was limited and over the next couple of years Hitler and the Nazis struggled to make their voices heard.

Hitler never gave up hope though. He knew deep down that his party would always struggle in the good times, but those good times could never last forever. Hitler spent this time reorganising his party and getting all of the old original members to buy in to his new party under his total control and leadership. Those men who refused to comply, such as Ernst Röhm, were pushed out. Despite a new speaking ban placed on Hitler that was to run until 1927 the membership numbers of the party grew steadily if unspectacularly. In 1927 the numbers were 72,000; in 1928 this had grown to 108,000 and on to 178,000 in 1929. The party was also reorganised into regional 'Gaus' or districts, each Gau mirrored a Reichstag constituency, Hitler was now concentrating on achieving control over Germany by the power of the vote rather than the power of a gun.

It wasn't going well though. In the elections of May 1928 the Nazi Party recorded 810,000 votes from a possible 31,000,000, just 2.6% of the vote. If he was ever going to challenge the establishment, Hitler needed a miracle.

That miracle occurred on 24 October 1929 when the New York stock market crashed and sent the world into financial meltdown.

Dancing on a volcano: The Wall Street Crash

On the face of it, the German economy of the late twenties wasn't in bad shape. However, Streseman knew the real facts of the situation. He knew it was a lot more fragile than most people would care to admit. It was hugely dependent on foreign loans, especially from the United States of America and if any of Germany's creditors decided to call in their loans, Germany would be in all sorts of problems. Most eloquently, Streseman likened it to Germany 'dancing on a volcano'.

In October 1929, that volcano erupted. Big time.

During the 'roaring twenties', America enjoyed years of sustained prosperity. As the economy grew, so did the stock market with millions of Americans wanting a piece of the stock market action. It was easy for the average American to have a slice of this particular pie – they didn't even need to have much disposable cash to sit at the table, they were able to borrow the money to buy their stocks based on the perceived value of the stocks in question – much like a mortgage on a house, however if the value of the stocks fell below the amount that had been borrowed against them, the borrower had to repay the loan amount in full and immediately. The debt accumulated in this fashion was obscene. It is estimated that by 1929 about six billion dollars of debt had been amassed in this way. Six billion dollars is a hell of a lot of money even today, but in 1929 that was a monumental pile of cash. Everything was going swimmingly, and would continue to do so as long as there was continued steady growth. However if stock values fell then the whole structure would be in danger of total collapse. But stocks could never fall in value could they. Could they?

On Thursday, 24 October 1929 the inevitable happened. Stock prices fell dramatically. Almost thirteen million shares were sold, twice the amount that had ever been sold before in one day. People were panicking. It was 'brown-trousers' time for a lot of American speculators.

Through frantic activity, the traders on Wall Street were able to temporarily reverse the decline over the next two days but on Tuesday 29 October stocks took another sharp dive as millions of stock owners decided to cut their losses and get what they could from their stocks. This time the traders were helpless to do anything. Everyone was selling, no one was buying and as a result, prices took an absolute beating. Over sixteen million shares were sold that day. It was a new record that no-one really wanted to be a part of.

The American banks now found themselves in a precarious position. Millions of Americans who had borrowed money from them to buy stocks that were now worthless could not pay back their loans. Immediately they knocked on the door of the Weimar Republic and gave it notice that they wanted the money back that they had loaned Germany over the last few years. It was a disaster for German industry and the Weimar Republic.

Very quickly Germany factories could no longer afford to keep their machines turning and German banks started to ship water at an alarming rate. Neither Britain, France or Russia were in a position to lend Germany any money, they were all still struggling to recover their own finances following the First World War. On top of this, a request for an economic union with Austria was quickly kicked into touch by the international community as it contravened the terms of the Treaty of Versailles.

Germany was on her own.

Organisations throughout Germany went bankrupt and workers were laid off in their millions. It was just six years after the problems of hyper-inflation, but yet again almost every German family was hit with acute financial uncertainty. By September 1930 there were three million unemployed in Germany, two years previous, that figure had been less than 700,000. In these harsh conditions it was no wonder that many Germans, who saw no real solution to their problems, started to listen to the more extreme political parties, such as the Nazis and the Communists.

The membership numbers of the Communist Party in Germany almost trebled between 1929 and 1932 and to many ordinary Germans the threat of a Communist revolution was very real. This obviously played right into the hands of right wing parties such as the Nazis who promised to rid the country of the evil Communists and protect the interest of the average German citizen.

General elections were held in September 1930, this would be Hitler's opportunity to truly make a stand. He embarked on an intense political campaign in the run up to the elections. His nationalistic rhetoric gave the desperate people of Germany hope. He promised them jobs, he promised them bread, he promised to rip up the Treaty of Versailles and make Germany a powerhouse once again.

The campaigning worked. The NSDAP secured almost 6.5 million votes. Compared to 810,000 votes in the previous election two years ago this was an impressive rise in fortunes. The Nazis went from being the smallest party in parliament to the second biggest.

Germany had just taken her first steps on the road to full-on dictatorship.

A Republic in Crisis: Elections 1932

Heinrich Brüning was made Chancellor by President Hindenburg in March 1930. He had a tough job as he was thrown straight into the teeth of the Great Depression. One of his main aspirations was to free the economy of the burden of the reparations – this should have made him a very popular Chancellor, but he went about it in an unpopular way – tight control on credit and large scale wage cuts.

Added to this, the elections of September 1930 delivered a very divided Reichstag (parliament). The Nazi Party had secured over 18% of the vote and the German Communist Party had gained over 13% of the vote. It seemed that the bulk of the German voters were gravitating towards the extremes of right and left. Brüning was the leader of the Catholic Centre Party and was caught slap in the middle of these two extremes.

This was a situation that would only end in tears.

The Nazis and the Communists fought (quite literally most of the time) like the proverbial cat and dog. Brüning found it almost impossible to control them and as a result democracy itself started to slowly crumble. During the 1920s the Reichstag met for business on average one hundred days a year. From April 1931 to July 1932 it met for only twenty-four days.

In an effort to get his way, Brűning began to issue emergency decrees under Article 48 of the German Constitution – effectively bypassing the Reichstag. The notion of an effective German democracy had begun to erode away long before Hitler sat in the top seat.

Brűning's main concern was of course the economy. He set about making some pretty harsh public funding cuts, many of which were deeply unpopular with the civilian population, not least the reorganisation of unemployment benefits, which left millions of long-term unemployed suffering significant drops in household income and over a million people with no unemployment benefit at all. Mix this with rising prices and increased taxes as Brűning tried to boost the country's coffers and it was easy to see how millions of Germans were becoming fed up with the Weimar Republic.

The term of presidency for Hindenburg came to an end in 1932 and, as he was at the ripe old age of eighty-four and not a lover of politics, he had intended to call it a day. However, with the news that a certain Adolf Hitler had succeeded in gaining German citizenship and had gone public with his intention of running for the top job he decided to run again. Hindenburg won the election with over nineteen million votes, but Hitler wasn't far behind with almost thirteen and a half million votes himself. He may have lost this particular election, but he had catapulted himself into the big time.

Decree after decree and dictatorial decision after dictatorial decision made Brűning the most unpopular chancellor in the Weimar's history. He was public enemy number one and he knew it. He resigned in May 1932 and was replaced by Franz von Papen, a German nobleman and an officer of the General Staff. Von Papen quickly surrounded himself with all of his old cronies and as a result quickly came under fire for being too disconnected with the issues faced by the general public. At the Reichstag elections of July 1932 the Nazi Party gained 37.4% of the vote and became the single biggest political party in Germany.

Not surprisingly Hitler marched straight into the office of President Hindenburg and demanded to be declared Chancellor. The President politely declined, citing he didn't feel comfortable handing power to a party that was intolerant, violent and lacking in discipline. The old man was a good judge of character.

Yet, a few months later, despite a dip in the popularity of the Nazi Party in the November elections and constant internal fighting, Adolf Hitler was named Chancellor of Germany by the self-same man that had categorically said 'Nein' in August that year.

As the saying goes: Good things come to he who waits.

Propaganda: The Nazi Political Machine

The reasons why so many people voted for the Nazi Party were numerous and varied. During the late twenties and early thirties the average German citizen was having a really tough time of it and in times of hardship people tend to listen more to reactionary and radical political voices. But the NSDAP wasn't the only right wing party in Germany, there were dozens of them to choose from. So this begs the question: Why the Nazis? Why Hitler?

Right from the beginning in the mid-twenties, Hitler had shown that he was never backwards in coming forwards. He was very smart when it came to PR and promotion – both for himself and his party – and very quickly put into practice a very structured, highly organised and hugely effective PR and propaganda machine. To illustrate his views on this subject, he wrote the following passage in Mein Kampf:

"The receptive powers of the masses are very restricted, and their understanding is feeble. On the other hand, they quickly forget. Such being the case, all effective propaganda must be confined to a few bare essentials and those must be expressed as far as possible in stereotyped formulas. These slogans should be persistently repeated until the very last individual has come to grasp the idea that has been put forward."

Just seventy words, but they would act as the bedrock of Nazi propaganda for the next twenty-odd years.

In 1930 a certain Joseph Goebbels was placed in charge of the propaganda arm of the NSDAP. An intelligent man (he held a PhD on nineteenth century literature from Heidelberg University) and an astute politician, he put together a fantastically organised and well-oiled machine that acted in a similar fashion to many large organisations today. Corporate messaging, information and instruction were developed by Party HQ and disseminated down to all local branches. These regional branches were allowed to adapt these messages to local requirements and they were also encouraged to submit ideas and solicit feedback.

The Nazis were also adept at tailoring their message to specific audiences, just like a professional and well-disciplined marketing department. Leaflets were specifically written, designed and produced to appeal to different members of society: farmers, shopkeepers, the unemployed, businessmen, financiers and factory workers all saw the principals of National Socialism in a slightly different way. It was all very clever.

Goebbels and his PR cronies were also pretty clued up when it came to the deployment of their messages and the vehicles they needed to use to get their message out to the public – they showed a decent understanding of the psychology of messaging – using strong simple imagery, and a clever use of colour helped ingrain their messages into the general population. They were also very quick to use new technologies and new techniques in the art of electioneering. Loudspeakers, video, radio and music were all used to further their cause. Image was important to them, they felt the need to portray the image of a proper political outfit that were worthy of the role of statesmen, so flash cars and even flasher private planes were hired to take the party leaders out on the road. Local events such as fairs, concerts or sporting events were hosted and proved popular and a great way to meet the electorate. In 1930s Germany, perception was reality and the Nazis knew it better than anyone.

All of this was brilliant electioneering and went a long way in positioning the party as a mainstream party of substance, yet there was one other thing that elevated the NSDAP way above every other political party; one thing that they did better than anyone else and which made a real tangible difference to their popularity at the ballot box.

The massed rally.

The whole idea of the mass rally was to create an atmosphere so charged with emotion that everyone present was swept up on a tidal wave of collective will and excitement that was almost impossible to resist. At these huge events the Nazis pulled out all the stops: uniforms, flags, music, lighting, songs, salutes, anthems, rousing speeches from their leaders. They used them all to great effect and there is no doubt thousands upon thousands of Germans were 'converted' at such rallies.

Power at last: Hitler becomes Chancellor

July 1932. Von Papen continued as Chancellor but without a majority in the Reichstag he was constantly up against it. He wasn't the only person who was getting frustrated though; Hitler was starting to get twitchy too. His party was obviously very popular with the German public but to date he was struggling to turn that popularity into the one thing he craved above all else.

Power.

Hindenburg and von Papen met with Hitler in August that year to see if he would accept a position of lesser authority as they were keen to have Nazi representation in the cabinet but reticent to give any of them the top seat. Not surprisingly, Hitler refused, for him it was all or nothing. The meeting ended in deadlock.

From August to December 1932 the Nazi Party suffered what could be described as a mini-crisis. Many members of the SA, especially the more 'radical' individuals, were getting increasingly restless, morale was on the slide throughout the party and when another round of elections were called in November there was a distinct possibility that they would run out of cash. These problems were not lost on the astute von Papen who hoped that by dissolving the Reichstag once more would he could undermine the Nazi position of strength within German politics.

To a certain degree he was correct. In the November elections the Nazi Party's vote declined to 11.7 million votes (33.1%) and as a result their numbers in the Reichstag were depleted too. However, most of these lost votes went to the Communist Party which meant they increased their share of the Reichstag and made the government even harder to manage than before. To make matters worse von Papen was also losing the support of the Army, a vital ally if he had any hope of banning the Communists and Nazis and ruling by decree.

After the elections a number of prominent industrial and financial leaders petitioned President Hindenburg asking him to appoint Hitler as Chancellor. They were becoming increasingly nervous of the growing Communist influence within Germany, and even though they may not have been fanatical Nazis themselves, they would support anyone if it meant kicking Communism out of their country. They were also fed up of the continuing elections which was having an adverse effect on the economy. They wanted an authoritarian approach to fixing Germany's problems and to be honest Adolf Hitler was the best of what was available. At least he was the leader of the largest national political party.

With nowhere to go and with no real support from any political or industrial corner, von Papen resigned in December 1932. Instead of offering something to Hitler, the Chancellorship was given to General von Schleicher and he offered the vice-Chancellorship to Gregor Strasser, leader of the north German wing of the Nazi Party. Strasser declined and actually walked away from his position in the Nazi Party, but not before putting the boot into Hitler about his obsession with power. Something he may have regretted eighteen months down the line when Hitler decided on having a 'clear out' of people that had annoyed him on his journey to becoming Führer.

It became quickly apparent that von Schleicher was having the same issue controlling the Reichstag as his predecessor. There was growing civil unrest throughout the country with the SA and the Communists having fun knocking seven bells out of each other on a regular basis in the streets. A secret research study was undertaken to assess the German Army's ability to effectively respond to a national emergency if things got completely out of control on the streets; the damning verdict was absolute in its findings. The Army was in no fit state to do anything. If it all kicked off in a major way between the Nazis and the Communists the Army would be powerless to do anything about it. This was perhaps the final straw. Germany was running out options.

On 4 January 1933 Hitler met von Papen to discuss the future. It was agreed that von Papen would lobby Hindenburg to allow Hitler to become Chancellor on the condition that von Papen would be Vice-Chancellor and there would be only two other Nazis in the cabinet. Hitler agreed.

The lobbying was successful and on the morning of 30 January 1933 Adolf Hitler was proclaimed Chancellor of Germany. He had made good on his promise by attaining power in a legal fashion and in doing so ended fourteen years of botched democracy under the Weimar Republic.

Von Papen was confident that with the help of Hindenburg and with the fact that only three cabinet seats out of a total of eleven were held by National Socialists, he would be able to control Hitler and dominate the cabinet, effectively ensuring he ran Germany.

He would be very disappointed.

Chaos and compliance: Towards a one party state

Yes, Hitler was now Chancellor of Germany, but in the beginning he was actually quite vulnerable. He reported directly to Hindenburg who could sack him at any given moment and the old man had already proven he wasn't afraid to act if he wasn't happy. He just had to ask von Papen, Brűning or von Schleicher about that. In truth Hitler was absolutely miles away from being a dictator and in his first months as Chancellor he worked hard to consolidate his position and authority. Within twenty-four hours of his appointment he convinced Hindenburg to announce new elections – with more industrial backers and a bigger national stage, Hitler was convinced he would get his majority.

Apart from Hitler, the Nazi Party occupied only two government posts in early 1933 but they were important and influential posts. Hermann Göring (a highly decorated WWI fighter pilot ace and a fanatical Nazi), in particular held a key post – that of Minister of the Prussian Interior – as it gave him control over the police force in the majority of Germany and he used and abused this power to ensure the police turned a blind eye to the activities of the SA and the SS and at the same time implored them (the Police) to deal ruthlessly with anyone who showed any kind of dissent against Hitler and the State. Göring also removed hundreds of Republican officials from key posts in Prussia and replaced them with Nazi Party members – often SA or SS members. If this wasn't enough Göring then put in place an auxiliary Police Force made of 50,000 men – the majority of which were again were made up of SA and SS men. These were specifically tasked to harass trade unions and Communists.

Police resources in Prussia, which made up two-thirds of the entire country, were now completely and utterly in the pocket of the Nazis. Anyone who showed the tiniest amount of public opposition to the Nazis was swiftly and often brutally dealt with by the police or the auxiliary force.

Having control of the police was one thing, but if Hitler had any hope of gaining total power he needed the backing of the armed forces. It just so happened that the new Minister of Defence, General Werner von Bomberg, was far more sympathetic to the Nazi ideal than von Papen gave him credit for. In an address to senior Army officers in February 1933 Hitler reaffirmed his commitment to restore conscription and to rip up the terms of the Treaty of Versailles. In return he wanted confirmation of Army neutrality (i.e. no interference) with regards to any political issues. He got his wish.

With the Army compliant the tide of Nazi violence against their competition was raised up a notch or two. At the end of January 1933 the SA and SS put on large triumphant parades in a show of power and confidence. Simultaneously the number of violent incidents and acts of anti-Semitism began to multiply significantly. The auxiliary force began to attack the trade union and Communist offices along with the homes of their leaders but with the agreements in place with the police the common situation was that the Communists/Jews/Trade Unionists would get a kicking from the Nazis and then be arrested and thrown in prison for breaches of the peace. Of course, none of the SA/SS storm troopers involved in the violence were handed any sentence at all.

Local and regional authorities, under the 'guidance' of Göring had begun to impose banning orders on the publication of Social Democrat newspapers – an action that was temporarily overturned in the courts, but the Nazis just sent 'the boys' round in the shape of gangs of Brownshirts (SA) to beat them all up.

All the time this was going on Goebbels and Hitler were winding up the German public, telling them that there was the real danger of a Communist uprising and a Bolshevik revolution and when it appeared the German public must be ready to stamp it out quickly and sharply in order to preserve the future of Germany.

Unfortunately this 'revolution' wasn't forthcoming. The Nazis had failed to provoke the Communists into action, it was time to revert to plan B – making stuff up.

On 24 February a group of Göring's 'police' raided the Communist Party HQ in Berlin, even though it had long been abandoned. Most if not all of the significant Communist politicians had either gone into hiding or had shuffled off to Russia to get out of the way and not surprisingly there wasn't much of interest left in the building, but they did find piles of old propaganda leaflets that had been left behind in the cellar. This was enough for Goebbels to announce that a large amount of 'seized documents' proved beyond doubt that the Communists were about to kick off and launch their much anticipated revolution.

The public and the rest of the government were not convinced. Goebbels needed something more. He needed stronger 'proof' that the Communists were actively plotting to bring down Germany. Then, on 27 February, the Reichstag building went up in flames.

Fire at the Reichstag

The fire alarms began to ring out into the Berlin night air at around 10pm on 27 February. A Dutch construction worker and Communist sympathiser Marinus van der Lubbe was arrested on site by Reichstag officials with matches, firelighters and Communist leaflets on his person. In the eyes of the police that arrested him and the watching crowds he was bang to rights guilty.

Hitler, Göring and Goebbels rushed to the scene as soon as they realised what was happening and quickly claimed that it was a 'Communist crime against the new government' and the start of the 'Communist revolution'.

Was the fire really started by Marinus van der Lubbe of his own volition or was he the Nazi equivalent of Lee Harvey Oswald? Was the fire actually started by members of the SA or SS in order for the Nazis to blame the Communists and give them a legitimate excuse to give them a public haranguing? The basic truth is that we will probably never know. In 1960, the German news magazine Der Spiegel organised a wide ranging investigation and backed the version of events trumpeted by the Nazis that Marinus van der Lubbe was guilty as charged, however in 2001 a bunch of historians begged to differ. After pouring over newly released documents from the East German and Soviet archives they concluded that the fire was actually a Nazi plot to frame the Communists and that the Der Spiegel investigation was nothing more than a cover up. This new argument is based on remarks made by a Nazi storm trooper named Adolf Rall who claimed that SA leader Karl Ernst ordered Rall and a group of SA men to enter the Reichstag via a tunnel and sprinkle flammable liquid inside. Rall's body was found in woods near Berlin in November 1933. Make of that what you will...

On 6 December 2007, the Attorney General of Germany posthumously pardoned van der Lubbe based on a 1998 German law that makes it possible to overturn certain cases of Nazi injustice.

The argument about who set the Reichstag on fire still rages, long after the flames of the fire in question have fizzled out. What is agreed though is that regardless of whoever did it, the Nazis played the situation perfectly to their advantage and grasped the opportunity to pass extremely draconian laws that allowed them to round up tens of thousands of their political opposition and give them an absolute hiding, before throwing the ones that survived into jail.

Hindenburg was persuaded to pass an emergency decree on 28 February 'for the protection of people and state'. The first paragraph of this new law restricted certain acts of personal freedom such as freedom of expression and the right of assembly, as well as restricting the privacy of the postal service and imposing significant restrictions on the press. The second paragraph gave central government the power to overrule regional governments. This law basically legalised the active suppression of all forms of political opposition. By whatever means necessary.

It was nothing more than a public demolition of the democratic constitution of the Weimar Republic and as such it proved to be the first step on Hitler's journey to outright dictatorship. By the end of April 1933 about 25,000 opponents of the Nazi regime had been rounded up in Prussia alone and either killed or put in prison.

A week later, on 5 March, the country went to the polls yet again. Surely this time, with Hitler as Chancellor, with the police in their pocket, and with thousands of their political opponents either dead or in jail, it was just a formality that the Nazis would get a landslide majority victory?

Actually, no.

Hitler and his boys did increase their share of the vote, from 33.1% to 43.9% but it was still some way short of the majority share Hitler so badly craved. He could only get that majority with the help of the 52 seats (8% of the votes) at the Reichstag that were in the possession of the Nationalists. As allies to the Nazis, the Nationalists gave the Nazis their seats and that got them 52% and an overall majority in parliament.

Now they were in business.

Nazi storm troopers seized control of local and city governments, by force if needed. By mid-March the swastika flag was fluttering above every single official government building in Germany. If any minister raised an objection they were forced to resign or arrested. Or both. Pro-Nazi officials were quickly established as replacements and within a matter of weeks the entire regional system of German government had been crushed – replaced by central control.

To handle all of the new influx of political prisoners, special camps were built. The first one was opened on 22 March 1933 and was quickly filled by so-called enemies of the state, even though most of them never faced trial. That first camp was situated in Dachau.

Soon these kinds of camps were sprouting up all over the country like evil mushrooms. At this time they were not the death camps that became synonymous with the Final Solution but they were still nasty places and the inmates were treated very badly. By the end of the year over 100,000 people were held in these concentration camps with several hundred being killed.

Gleichschaltung: The Enabling Act

Despite not having a true majority, Hitler pressed on with his grand plan. He went ahead and proposed a new Enabling Act that would effectively transfer all law making powers directly to him as Chancellor, technically giving him a legalised dictatorship, signed and sealed by the Reichstag.

In order to win this vote, Hitler needed the support of the conservative centre and centre-right and in an attempt to get their support the Nazis put on a huge show of nationalism in an effort to reassure and appease their would be allies.

In front of many German dignitaries including Hindenburg and the Crown Prince, Goebbels organised an ornate and extravagant ceremony that was broadcast to the nation in the Potsdam Garrison Church on 21 March to celebrate the opening of the new Reichstag and to align the cause of National Socialism to the old German way.

The whole event was very tightly choreographed; the town of Potsdam was chosen for its special place in German history. Frederick the Great had transformed this tiny region into a powerful state back in the eighteenth century – mainly through military achievement. Hitler and Hindenburg made powerful speeches, Hitler made no reference to his hatred of Communism or the Jews, he made no reference to his racial ideology, he made no reference or threat to anyone or any country. Instead he preached about re-affirming the traditions of Germany and the importance of a firm government. Flags were flown, cannons were fired, wreaths were laid and prayers were said. Even the date of the event, the first day of spring, was laced with subconscious messages about a fresh start, of growth and renewal. It was an emotionally charged day.

Two days later the Reichstag met in the Kroll Opera House to consider the Enabling Act. On that day the party put forward a very different image. The Communists (what were left of them) were refused entry to the building and the rest of the non-Nazi government officials were met with a torrent of intimidation. Unruly crowds had gathered outside and many of the politicians had to run a gauntlet of hate and abuse just to get inside the building. Once inside they were met by hundreds of angry looking armed SS and SA men who were prowling the halls and corridors, covered in swastika flags and associated ornaments. There was no denying who was in charge.

Before the vote Hitler took to the microphone once more, re-affirming his stance of a strong safe government and even promising to fully respect the rights of the Catholic Church and to uphold all religious and moral values. These last statements were lies and were purely mentioned to gain the support of the Centre Party. They worked though, and the Enabling Act was passed by 444 votes to 94. In the end only the Social Democrats had attempted to stop the Nazis.

The turkey's had effectively voted for Christmas. Hitler could now make laws without needing the agreement of the Reichstag or the President. He was free to march down the road to a one party totalitarian dictatorship.

Once secure, Hitler wasted no time in bringing many parts of Germany 'into line' (Gleichschaltung). Germany had historically possessed a very strong and influential trade union movement which had tight links with ideologies such as socialism and catholicism and not surprisingly these trade unions were seen as a large threat to the stability of the Nazi state. On 2 May 1933 trade union buildings across Germany were occupied by the SA and the SS. All trade union leaders were arrested and their unions were immediately swallowed up by the Nazi run DAF (Deutscher Arbeitsfront – German Labour Front). In a matter of days independent trade unions had ceased to exist.

On 10 May all assets and funds belonging to the Social Democrats were seized. Six weeks later the party was banned. On 1 July an agreement was made with the Roman Catholic Church which promised that the government would not interfere with Catholic affairs on one condition: the abolition of the Catholic Centre Party. The Church agreed and the Catholic Centre Party became extinct on 5 July 1933.

On 14 July the Communist Party was banned and with them the entire left wing of the German political spectrum had been eradicated. The so called 'allies' of the Nazis were not safe either. The leader of the Nationalists was banned from speaking in July and was subjected to numerous personal attacks by the pro-Nazi press. He quickly got fed up and resigned, and with that his party crumbled to dust.

By mid-summer 1933 the process of Gleichschaltung was working beautifully: the Reichstag was irrelevant, the police were in the pocket of the Nazis, the Communists were crushed, all the other parties were banned and anyone of any significance who opposed the regime was locked up in concentration camps. In the public sector, all Jewish civil servants had been sacked (apart from those who had served in the First World War or whose fathers had served) and all remaining civil servants had to greet each other with the 'Hitler Salute'.

In six short months Hitler had transformed the face of Germany but it wasn't quite the insatiable orgy of sauerkraut and jackboots that Hitler wanted. He was still not 100% secure in his position as Chancellor. He could still be sacked by President Hindenburg and he could still be overthrown by the Army if they got too fed up with his antics, or more to the point, the antics of the SA.

The SA had grown almost uncontrollably over the last year or so. It was unruly, it was violent and it was royally pissing off the middle classes. Worse still, the Army had started to make noises that suggested it thought the SA was getting a bit too big for its boots – these kind of murmurings worried Hitler, he could not afford to alienate the Army.

It was time to put the issue of the SA to bed once and for all.

Gotcha! The Night of the Long Knives

Hitler gave a speech on 6 July 1933 warning of the dangers of keeping Germany in a constant state of revolution. He wanted an end to the random and continuous violence on the streets. Now.

The behaviour of many party activists worried him. Some of the more extreme party members were in danger of becoming a political embarrassment for him as he tried to consolidate his position as the head of a serious political regime and the leader of his country. His speech on that July day was nothing more than a thinly veiled threat that all Nazis needed to accept the realities and responsibilities of being a grown up full time political party.

The speech failed. In fact it only served to exacerbate the fears of the ordinary Nazi that their leadership was softening their stance on some of their most fundamental ideals. There began calls for a second, more radical revolution, hell bent on destroying the German establishment through force. The majority of these calls came from the ranks of the SA.

The SA (Sturmabteilung – Storm Division) had been a fixture of the Nazi Party right from the very beginning. Kitted out in ex-WWI light brown uniforms originally produced for the German Army serving in Africa (hence their nickname of the

'Brownshirts') many of the early members were veterans of the war. Originally known as the 'Hall Defence Detachment' they were initially tasked with protecting the political meetings of the DAP (as they were then called) and breaking up the meetings of rival parties. It wasn't until a particularly violent fight in November 1921 that they took on the name the Sturmabteilung. After the failed Munich putsch in 1923 the SA was effectively banned. Ernst Röhm was the leader in those days but after a number of arguments with Hitler he left Germany in 1925 to be an advisor to the Bolivian Army.

Over the next few years the SA proved a troublesome bunch. Often rebelling and always getting into fights. The SS (Schutzstaffel – Protection Squad) was formed in 1925 and originally functioned as a small body guard detachment for Adolf Hitler, but after Heinrich Himmler was appointed the leader of the SS in January 1929 he put in place a plan to build up the membership of the SS whom he saw as superior to the Brownshirts. This put several senior SA leaders' noses out of joint – they did not like the SS one little bit as they saw it as a rival to their power and influence within the Nazi Party. On one occasion a unit of SA men attacked Goebbels' office and beat up his SS bodyguards. In an effort to calm the SA down, Hitler recalled Röhm in 1931. By 1934 the membership of the SA had reached over four million men.

In February 1934 Röhm presented to the cabinet his idea that the SA, the SS, and the armed forces should be merged under a single Ministry of Defence organisation, which, indecently, he himself should be in charge of. The generals couldn't think of anything worse. The whole glorious tradition of the German Army would be destroyed if a rough-neck like Röhm got his hands on it. No. And in any case, there were rumours circulating concerning widespread corruption and homosexuality at the SA top table and the German Army would not be involved in any of that kind of nonsense, thank you very much.

Tensions between the Army and the SA grew steadily worse during 1934 with numerous clashes between Röhm and the Army generals. In March the Minister of Defence suggested to Hitler that he thought that the SA were secretly arming themselves and getting ready for their own revolution. The Army was getting increasingly fed up with the antics of Röhm and his Brownshirts, Hitler had to do something to appease them. Fast.

His opportunity came in April 1934 on board the cruiser Deutschland as Hitler joined Army and Navy commanders on spring maneuvers. On board they all discussed the impending death of the old President who was currently gravely ill. Hitler knew that the army generals all favoured a return to a monarchy system, something which he himself was not overly keen on! He wanted to be President and in return for the unreserved support of the military in his quest for the Presidency he promised to sort out the 'problem' of the SA once and for all. Both the Army and the Navy agreed unanimously and unreservedly to support Hitler as the rightful successor to President Hindenburg.

It was the last piece of the puzzle for Hitler, his path to total dictatorship was now clear.

As Germany approached the summer of 1934, all was not rosy in the Nazi garden. The infighting between Röhm, Goering and Himmler was becoming more and more intense. Röhm had been forced to sign a declaration promising to respect the independence of the armed forces but soon local SA detachments were beginning to seize arms and ammo. It looked like the SA were indeed about to kick off big time, although there was no real coordinated plan. Ultimately that 'second revolution' never materialised. But that didn't stop other high ranking Nazis distancing themselves from the Brownshirts. Both Himmler and Göring were secretly building personal police forces of their own and with Göring being appointed an infantry general by Hindenburg, he started to distance himself from the SA and even threw away his brown uniform.

In early June von Papen spoke out about the 'second revolution' criticising it very strongly. This infuriated Hitler but because of how influential von Papen was he had to take heed of his words. A few days later Hitler visited the gravely ill President – it was becoming very clear that the President was seriously considering pushing Hitler aside and instigating military rule in Germany if the SA issue wasn't sorted out.

Hitler was being pressurised by three sides to take action against the SA; the President, the Army and also his own colleagues in Himmler and Göring were nagging him to do something. Himmler and his deputy, Reinhard Heydrich had put together a complete dossier of manufactured facts that 'proved' that Röhm had been paid millions to kick Hitler out of office. That was the last straw, there was no other choice, Röhm had to go.

On 30 June 1934 Röhm and other main SA leaders were rounded up by members of the SS. Most were shot immediately but Röhm was taken to Stadelheim Prison in Munich and encouraged to commit suicide. He refused and was later shot on 2 July. The killings were not limited to just SA leaders, across Germany old political rivals were murdered too including Gregor Strasser who had annoyed Hitler in 1932 by resigning from the party. Kurt von Schleicher – a former Chancellor, Gustav Ritter von Kahr – the man who crushed the Munich Putsch as well as a number of von Papen's staff were also taken care of. All in all, hundreds of opponents past and present were hacked to death, shot, stabbed or hung by the SS in what became known as the 'Night of the Long Knives.

The SA would never recover as a potent political force. The second revolution had been averted.

Der Fűhrer

Hindenburg remained in his position as President until the very last, but on 2 August 1934 the great old man passed away at his home in Neudeck, East Prussia. He was eighty-six. With his passing, Hitler declared that the role of President would be permanently vacant. In effect Hitler became both Chancellor and President under a new title.

Der Fűhrer

On 19 August Hitler asked the German population to vote and ratify his position as the head of the two top jobs in Germany. 84.6% voted yes, it was an overwhelming show of support. The country wanted Hitler to lead them into a bright future.

Actually, it wasn't as overwhelming as the raw statistics would have you believe. Despite the lack of opposition, despite the Nazi controlled police, despite the intimidation, the beatings, the concentration camps, despite all of this over 15% of Germans actually had the guts to say no. Regionally the variances were wide, in some areas the 'yes' vote was as low as 66%.

Clearly, not everyone approved of Der Fűhrer.

Regardless, Hitler had now been voted in as Germany's head of state and head of government. By default he was also

Commander-in-Chief of the armed forces all of whom were now compelled to swear an oath to Hitler personally. With the Army in his pocket along with the police, and no real opposition, his hold on power was finally secure.

Adolf Hitler was now master of all Germany.

A cultural revolution

On 13 March 1933 Hitler's government introduced the Reich Ministry for Popular Enlightenment and Propaganda. The position of top man for this new department, and with it a seat in the cabinet, went to a man who had impressed Hitler with his inventive and creative propaganda campaigns in Berlin in recent years.

Dr Joseph Goebbels.

Ten days later, Hitler himself outlined the plans for this new Ministry: "The government will embark upon a systematic campaign to restore the nation's moral and material health. The whole educational system, theatre, film, literature, the press, and broadcasting – all these will be used as a means to this end. They will be harnessed to help preserve the eternal values which are part of the integral nature of our people."

What Hitler was talking about here was the fact that in his eyes the majority of Germans, i.e. those people that didn't vote Nazi in the last election, had been brain-washed and psychologically 'altered' by the devious and scandalous acts of Jewish Bolshevism. The 'Jewish-dominated' press and media, the Jewish art and music movements and other similar un-German sects had somehow misguided many millions of Germans to move away from their true and traditional German inner self.

And it was down to the government to fix that on behalf of the people. After all, Dr Goebbels knows best, right?

The removal of Jews from cultural society was seen as a priority for the Nazis as they thought they had completely undermined traditional German values – as such the new Ministry was granted almost cart blanche autonomy from Hitler to enable them to do whatever they needed to do to fix the problem. This meant that Goebbels had the power to override any objections that may come from rival departments that may arise from his or his department's actions, he set about his first task: to destroy what he termed 'cultural Bolshevism'.

In music, all of the composers that were deemed to be 'un-German' were banned, they even tried to ban jazz and the playing of the saxophone, but they failed to do so. They had more luck with the press though; all newspapers that refused to follow the party line were banned, and by April 1933 the journalists' trade union was put under Nazi control, as was the German Publishers' Association. Soon there was just one German daily newspaper distributed across the entire nation – the Party's own rag – jovially called the Racial Observer – the Nazis made little or no effort to hide their racial agenda. It was a vital propaganda tool and a great way to tell the German population what to say, what to do and what to think. In 1932 the paper's circulation was just over 115,000 but by the middle of the Second World War it had shot up to over 1.1 million. The copy inside was bigoted, triumphant, arrogant, inciteful and threatening to anyone who dared to question the Nazi Party, but there was very little else to read. By 1939 the publishing house that ran the Racial Observer owned or controlled two thirds of the entire stock of German newspapers and magazines.

In June that year all radio broadcasting was brought under the direct authority of the new Ministry – Goebbels sacked almost 15% of the broadcasting workforce almost immediately because they were Jewish. One month later the Reich Film Chamber was set up to oversee and control all German film making. Not surprisingly any actor, director or producer who was Jewish or whose face didn't fit for whatever reason was quickly relieved of his or her duties.

By summer 1933 the press, radio and film industries were completely under Nazi control. Even Mickey Mouse was banned. The Nazi's cultural revolution was bouncing along nicely.

Writers, playwrights and artists were next on the hit list, many left Germany as they saw their works burned, banned or both. Painters whom Hitler disliked were banished from the Academy of Art, some were even revoked citizenship (a bit rich coming from an Austrian painter) and hundreds of art exhibitions were closed down as being 'un-German'.

Art museum directors that happened to be Jewish or Social Democrat or liberal or anything but hardcore Nazi were sacked and replaced by more 'informed' individuals that would ensure their properties only displayed artwork that received a nod of approval by the cultural regime. As the crackdown on artworks intensified, Goebbels issued a decree banning art criticism and in 1938 a law promoting the confiscation of items of 'degenerate art' was passed – this affected not only galleries and museums, but also private collections – thousands of pieces of artwork were taken by force, culminating in 1939 in almost 5,000 oil paintings, watercolours, drawings and other graphical work being burnt in the courtyard of Berlin's central fire station.

Writers didn't escape the crackdown either. All over the country bookshops and libraries were raided by the Gestapo, the police, local authorities, the Hitler Youth, the SA or anyone else that fancied bashing up a couple of retail outlets. Books by Jews, pacifists, Communists and anyone else that were deemed as unfit for consumption were taken and destroyed. In their place were books written by approved authors on approved topics. Perhaps not surprisingly, the 'heroic Aryan' overcoming many adversaries to save the world from the evil Jewish baddy was a very common fiction plot in the Germany of the thirties. On 10 May 1933 there was a mass book-burning session in all university towns up and down the country and shortly afterwards hundreds of titles were officially blacklisted

By the end of 1938 the Nazis enjoyed almost blanket control of German media. Intense Nazification of everything from newspapers to radio to music to plays to books meant that whatever citizens read, listened to, or looked at, the message they received had been approved by the Propaganda Ministry.

www.brainwashed.de

homeless. All were picked up and carted off to the nearest concentration camp.

One group of people that were considered to be actively polluting Germanic racial purity was the gypsies. The Nuremberg Laws of 1935 were later amended to include gypsies as well as Jews that were banned from marrying ethnic Germans and in December 1938 Himmler issued a memo to the police ordering them to ensure all gypsies over the age of six register at their local police office, the details of which were forwarded on to the Reich Central Office for Combatting the Gypsy Nuisance.

Despite all of this, it wasn't until the outbreak of war when the Nazis really started to get on the backs of the gypsy community. Thousands were rounded up and sent to concentration camps in Austria and by the end of the Nazi regime some 250,000 gypsies had been killed in the name of cleansing the German race.

Another group of people that irked the Nazis was homosexuals. Even though there was a high level of homosexual activity amongst the SA, especially in the early days, the Nazis had a very strong stance on this kind of behaviour. Hitler had Ernst Röhm shot because of his sexual orientation – although Hitler had known about it for a while and it only became an issue when he was looking for an excuse to get rid of him. Himmler was equally strict with his SS chaps, anyone caught was expelled and often shot.

In Nazi Germany it was illegal to be homosexual and the police had wide ranging powers which ultimately led to the arrest of 100,000 men, many of which were thrown into concentration camps where they were identified by a pink triangle sewn into their prison uniform. Inside these camps these inmates were often subjected to crude medical experiments in an effort to 'cure' them of their apparent disease. Many were castrated.

Economic transformation or a cunning ruse?

On 27 June 1933 the Reichstag issued a law authorising the design and construction of a new type of road.

The autobahn.

These long, wide motorways would link the major cities of Germany, enabling a communications link that would allow people, freight and produce to be transported across the country with unprecedented speed and convenience. Hitler himself was a huge petrol-head and loved travelling around by car and got very involved in the mapping of the autobahns to make sure they went through the most scenic areas of the country. On 23 September Hitler dug the first ceremonial piece of grass to signify the beginning of the construction of the first autobahn and by May 1935 the first section was open and by the summer of 1938, 3,500 kilometres of autobahn had been completed.

With tax incentives on car ownership, the motor vehicle industry blossomed – car manufacturing doubled between 1932 and 1933 and again by 1935 and hundreds of thousands of men were now employed either building roads or building cars or car components.

Indeed huge building projects such as the autobahns, new public buildings, draining of marshlands and transforming brownfield sites to agriculture had a massively positive affect on unemployment; in 1933 there were about six million people looking for work, by 1938 this figure had fallen to under one million.

As well as these monster construction projects, the Nazis also aggressively pursued a policy of getting as many people out of the labour market, especially women, as possible. Incentives for young wives to give up work were common place. The Nazis were strong proponents of women being the home maker and even proclaimed the idea of women working full time as being the invention of 'Jewish intellectuals'.

All of this industrial renovation provided the perfect groundwork for Hitler's ultimate goal for Germany.

Re-armament.

Hitler believed that these new factories, especially the automotive ones, could easily be converted to military production at short notice and the profits from these automotive manufacturers could be re-invested into developing tank and aero engines and running gear. He also believed that getting large numbers of German men back into work, especially manual work, would toughen them up and get them ready for the day when they became soldiers.

In the name of re-armament, thousands of factories were earmarked for military production. In the beginning these extra orders would just take up the slack in production due to the depression but soon the demands of the military machine forced significant investment.

The factories building the armour had to be careful in their paperwork as technically the Treaty of Versailles banned the production of any kind of gun, weapon, armoured vehicle or plane. In July 1933 the manufacturer Krupps started work on a large project involving 'agricultural tractors' – they were actually tanks. Thousands of military aircraft were built, many of which initially started out life as passenger planes but were quickly modified to become bombers. Soon factories all over Germany were churning out ships, rifles, ammunition, artillery and other military equipment creating tens of thousands of new jobs.

Paying for all this in the traditional way, i.e. via the government, would have raised alarm bells in the world community. To counter this and to keep the re-armament quiet the German government created credit notes using a cover organisation called the Metallurgical Research Corporation (abbreviated in German to MEFO). These MEFO bills were given to the factories by the government as form of payment and could be cashed in at any time, although the factories were encouraged to delay cashing them in due to the interest each MEFO earned them. By 'paying' for their guns in this way the government was able to fund huge manufacturing expansion with minimal financial outlay – meaning the whole business of arming Germany under the noses of the international community was kept practically invisible.

Genius.

Actually, no. On the face of it, Germany under the Nazis was experiencing magical economic growth, however there is always a trade-off when it comes to economics. In this case the trade-off was that the gross debt of the country was threatening to spiral out of control. Not that Hitler was bothered with that, he was convinced that this way of financing was only a short term measure and all of the debt would be cleared via territorial expansion in the near future.

One of the fundamental ideologies of the Nazi regime was to make Germany self-sufficient and not reliant on any other country for the importation of raw materials or food. The pain of the Allied blockade during the First World War was still raw for many and Hitler did not want to see a repeat. As a result he instructed Göring to set up a 'Four Year Plan' to make Germany self-sufficient by 1940. The Four Year Plan contained some radical ideas such as replacing imported raw materials with synthetic products made locally and incentives for farmers who increased food production. There were some successes; by 1939 Germany was self-sufficient in bread, potatoes, sugar and wheat, but ultimately the Plan failed. By the end of the 1930s Germany simply couldn't afford to import enough food and raw materials legitimately to keep it going. Germany needed more land so she could produce enough food for the population and raw materials to keep the factories busy. There was nothing else to do but invade and plunder.

For Hitler, war was the cure to all of his problems.

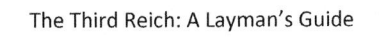

1935: Dismantling Versailles

When Hitler became Chancellor in 1933 he inherited a German nation that was weak and vulnerable on the international stage. Her armed forces were significantly depleted under the Treaty of Versailles, economically she was on her knees, and her constitution was in complete chaos. Germany then, was very vulnerable and it was no surprise that Hitler was very keen to talk up peace at every opportunity in his first few years in office. He knew that if anything naughty started in Europe, Germany was a sitting duck and could be invaded on a whim by anyone who fancied it. In May 1933 he actually called for other major European nations to be disarmed – although this was more than a bit cheeky seeing as he was actually committed to re-arming Germany as quickly as possible. But when France refused to disarm he took the opportunity to swiftly remove Germany from the League of Nations (the organisation tasked with upholding the terms of the Treaty of Versailles). In 1934 Hitler also signed a non-aggression pact with Poland, which was not worth the paper it was written on, but it served a purpose as it quelled Polish anxieties and at the same time managed to slightly calm the French, both of whom were still nervous of German expansion. Whilst conducting all of these peace talks, Hitler was setting the wheels in motion to build up Germany's armed defences as quietly and as secretly as possible.

One of the first things Hitler did once in power was to order the army to get recruiting. He gave them a target of trebling their numbers to 300,000 men by October 1934. German army officer lists were withdrawn from public circulation in an effort to hide the increases in staff and no-one in government or in the upper echelons of the army were allowed to discuss this expansion in public. Secrecy was the key.

More men would not win any kind of battle unless they had a few guns to play with. Luckily for Germany the gun makers and armament factories in the Ruhr had actually continued to churn out weapons since the twenties, right under the noses of the Allies. Submarines were clandestinely built in international ship building yards in Holland, Finland and Spain, and Hermann Göring, as Minister of Aviation, oversaw the League of Air Sports which was a cover department for the training of military pilots. Civil aviation organisations were asked to get thinking on war plane designs... just in case.

The first cracks in the Treaty of Versailles appeared in January 1935 when the Saarland, a piece of land in south-west Germany that was given to France for fifteen years as part of the terms of the Treaty, went to the ballot boxes to decide whether to stay as part of France or return to Germany. The public of the German speaking Saar region voted overwhelmingly to re-join Germany – almost 91% of those that cast their vote said 'ja' to joining the ranks of the Third Reich.

It was a massive coup for the Third Reich and the implications for German speaking minorities in other areas of Europe such as Czechoslovakia and Poland were obvious. The results in the Saarland also gave Hitler the confidence to publicly stick two fingers up at the Allies and the Treaty of Versailles. On 16 March 1935 Hitler announced to the world that he had re-established conscription to allow a peacetime army of around half a million men – this was five times the size permitted under the terms of the Treaty of Versailles. Not content with that, Hitler also declared the existence of the German Air Force. The next day there was a massive military procession through the streets of Berlin.

It was time for him to see what the rest of Europe was made of.

The answer was 'not a lot'. France and Britain grumbled and moaned but didn't actually do anything to stop the military expansion of Germany. Indeed just three months later Britain signed a Naval Agreement with Germany that allowed a German Navy to exist legally as long as it was only 35% of the size of the Royal Navy fleet. Another page of the Treaty of Versailles was technically ripped up and placed on the Nazi fire.

Hitler's gamble had paid off; the dismantling of the Treaty was well under way. Next in his sights was the demilitarised zone of the Rhineland.

The Rhineland

Towards the end of 1935 Benito Mussolini ordered the Italian invasion of Abyssinia, one of the last independent African states. Hitler watched with interest as Britain and France did absolutely nothing of note to stop Mussolini in his tracks. Italy was simply allowed to get away with it, thus proving the complete incompetence of the League of Nations to act on any international incident of this nature.

It was in the middle of this mini-crisis in Europe that Hitler decided to invade the Rhineland.

It was a huge risk and a decision that Hitler had been mulling over for months. He didn't have a massive invasion force to call upon and he was worried that the French would turn round and squash his army and maybe even retaliate in stronger fashion. Many of his army generals were opposed to the move for the same reason, however he made the decision to invade on 1 March 1936 and General Blomberg, the Minister of War and Commander-in-Chief, issued orders for the immediate occupation of the Rhineland.

It was game on.

On 7 March a token force of just three infantry battalions marched into the demilitarised zone. They were under orders to beat a hasty retreat if the French started to show any kind of sign of wanting a fight, but no such signs were forthcoming. Later that day Hitler stood triumphantly in front of an ecstatic Reichstag where he proclaimed:

"Men of the German Reichstag! In this historic hour, when, in the Reich's western provinces, German troops are marching into their future peacetime garrisons, we all unite in two sacred vows. First, we swear to yield to no force whatsoever in restoration of the honour of our people. Secondly, we pledge that we have no territorial demands to make in Europe! Germany will never break the peace!"

In the Reichstag that day it was a long time before the cheering finally stopped.

But not everyone was deliriously happy. Many of the army top brass were still very worried. Their troops were very vulnerable and there was still the distinct possibility that France would wake up and smash their tiny force to smithereens. The majority of the Army Generals wanted to pull their boys out. They had made their point, perhaps it was best to quit while they were ahead.

But Hitler was not for quitting.

He overruled his Generals and kept his forces where they were. The feared French counter-attack did not materialise. Not only did Hitler score a huge symbolic victory, he also 'proved' his judgment in military and foreign affairs was superior to his army commanders, feeding his ego even further and convincing him that in times of crisis, only he, with his iron will and nerves of steel, could make the right decision and save the day.

Hindsight is a wonderful thing, but It is fair to say that if the German push into the Rhineland had been swiftly dealt with there and then Hitler would have thought twice, even thrice, about any other excursions into neighbouring territory. Maybe the annexation of Austria, and the invasions of Czechoslovakia and Poland would not have happened. We will never know. What we do know, however is that because of the perceived victory in the Rhineland Hitler was lauded as a hero. When the German people were asked to vote on the topic of remilitarisation a whopping 98.8% voted in agreement with Hitler's decision. Germany approved.

The Treaty of Versailles now lay in tatters and with it went the final opportunity for France and Britain to stop, with minimal aggravation, the rise of an angry and highly militarised German nation.

Too late Too late will be the cry, when the last chance for peace in Europe passes you by...

1938: Pressing the pedal to the metal

Hitler, as one would expect from a man of his stature and status, attended and presided over a lot of meetings. He didn't really 'do' detail and many people seem to think that many of his major decisions were taken on the fly, using gut instinct rather than factual analysis of the situation. He was an opportunist, a good one, but not much of a strategist.

This may well be true, but there was one meeting that took place in November 1937 that shows sometimes had did indeed have a forward plan. In that meeting (it lasted about four hours) Hitler outlined to a few chosen senior officers and von Neurath (Foreign Minister) his plan for the next couple of years. The notes of the meeting were jotted down in what became known as the 'Hossbach Memorandum', imaginatively named after the chap who wrote down the notes during the meeting – a Colonel Hossbach.

During that meeting Hitler explained that the only way Germany could ever become self-sufficient would be to take large tracts of land from countries such as Austria, Poland and Czechoslovakia, however he feared that Britain and France would oppose such Germanic expansion and therefore the only way of going about it would be by using force. Hitler pledged to solve this problem of space for Germany once and for all by 1943-5. For him, the time for action had come – Austria and Czechoslovakia must be occupied ASAP and plans for the occupation of Poland and Russia should also be prepared.

It was time.

1938 turned out to be a big year for the Nazi regime. They not only turned on the afterburners of their foreign policy with quick and decisive occupations of both Austria and Czechoslovakia, but at home in Germany they also pressed the pedal to the metal.

Göring was placed in the driving seat of the economy, replacing Schacht, and von Neurath lost his post as Foreign Minister to Joachim von Ribbentrop – a hard-line Nazi and former German Ambassador to Britain. General von Blomberg was forced to resign as Minister for War when police records came to light suggesting that his wife had once posed for some risqué pictures. Not long after this scandal, Himmler and Göring 'found' evidence that seemed to indicate the current Commander-in-Chief of the Army, Colonel-General von Fritsch was up to no good with rent boys. He was actually innocent of all accusations, but such details seemed to matter little to the Nazi hierarchy and he too was removed from his post. Hitler took the opportunity to scrap the position of Minister for War and decided he himself was the best man for the job of running the Army.

Interestingly, both von Blomberg and von Fritsch were staunch opponents of Germany getting into a fight with France and Britain. Coincidence? It's unlikely.

Sixteen other generals whom Hitler deemed to be 'problematic' were 'retired' in 1938, along with another forty-four who were transferred to different posts. Without these old timers getting in his way, Hitler was clear to put into practice what he had preached during that meeting in November.

He wanted Austria, and he wanted her now.

Anschluss: March 1938

Kurt von Schuschnigg was no fool. The Chancellor of Austria knew that the Nazis wanted to exert more and more influence in his country, and to his credit he resisted as much as he could. In 1936 he bent a little as he signed an agreement that declared Austria to be a German state, but part of the agreement to signing was that Austria remained free, running independently of Germany. But as 1937 gave way to 1938 the pressure on Austria to become fully subservient to the Fatherland was becoming intense.

In early 1938 von Schuschnigg was summoned to Berchtesgaden to meet with Hitler. As soon as he arrived for the meeting, Hitler jumped on von Schuschnigg and put in front of him a list of demands he had of Austria, including reorganising the Austrian cabinet to ensure it was full of Nazis (including Arthur Seyss-Inquart, a promising lawyer and Austrian Nazi, who was to be made Austrian Minister of Security) and that Austrian economic and foreign policy be fully integrated into that of Germany.

He was given seven days to comply with the request.

On returning to Vienna, Schuschnigg decided to put the subject of Austrian independence from Germany to a referendum. Hitler was less than impressed and demanded that the vote be cancelled; he was also quick to approve military plans for the invasion of Austria that had been drawn up by General Keitel. Hitler knew that from intelligence gained by von Ribbentrop that Britain was unlikely to pick up the sword in defence of Austria, so all he had to do was convince Italy that her borders would be in no danger if an invasion took place. In the end an invasion wasn't needed. On 16 February the Austrian government announced a newly organised cabinet as well as a general amnesty for convicted Nazis even if they had been locked up for murder. Over the next four weeks a combination of agitation, intense military pressure and heightened propaganda succeeded in Hitler taking complete control of Austria with minimal fuss. Hitler rode triumphantly into the newest part of his Reich on 12 March.

The scene that greeted him that day was wild. The locals were delirious, they screamed, they cried, they threw flowers, they chanted, they saluted. It seemed to the entire world that the entire country of Austria had come to meet and greet their saviours. The Nazis.

Yet, it wasn't all rose petals and tea parties. Himmler and his SS boys were quick to get organised and immediately started 'cleansing' the country of any opposition. Jews were to get 'special' treatment; they were beaten, robbed, assaulted and forced to scrub the streets. Shops ran by Jewish Austrians were smashed to bits and ransacked. Tens of thousands were jailed, their possessions confiscated. The lucky ones were able to negotiate with the newly formed 'Office for Jewish Immigration' set up by Reinhard Heydrich but run and administered by Adolf Eichmann. This agency became the only place that would authorise permits to Jews to leave the country – often only in exchange for all of their worldly goods. The agency would soon morph, not into one for immigration, but one for extermination.

Very soon it became obvious that it was too much hassle to transport 'enemies' to concentration camps in Germany, Austria needed one for herself. To this end, a huge camp was built in the north of the country at Mauthausen. Over the next six or seven years this camp would cultivate itself a thoroughly nasty reputation for murder.

But right now, that was not a concern of Hitler or any of his senior Nazi colleagues. On 10 April Austria went to the ballot boxes to ratify the Anschluss in a referendum. For all who looked on from the outside, the vote looked all fair and square, but in reality it was anything but. The Nazis were past masters at intimidating and 'persuading' voters to put the X in their particular box, and this vote was no exception. It would have taken either a very brave or very stupid person to vote 'Nein' in this particular ballot. In the end over 99% of Austrians voted for the Anschluss.

There it was in black and white, ratified by the masses. Hitler had managed to increase the Reich by about seven million subjects without firing a shot. Austria ceased to exist and he had the ideal springboard to launch an attack on his next victim.

Czechoslovakia.

Case Green: Czechoslovakia

With Austria taken care of, the western side of Czechoslovakia was surrounded on three sides by German occupied territories. The country of Czechoslovakia was everything that Hitler hated; firstly it was created by the peace treaties that followed the First World War, secondly it was democratically run and rather prosperous to boot. Then there was the small matter of three and a half million Germans that lived in the Czech border state of Sudetenland. Hitler was determined to bring those Sudeten Germans under the wing of his blossoming empire.

To be fair, the Sudeten Germans weren't having a bad life. They were certainly doing better than many of the other minority groups living in Czechoslovakia. However Hitler would not be denied and set about stirring up trouble. The local Sudeten German Party had long been in the pocket of the Nazis, and now they were encouraged to start making noises about breaking from Czechoslovakia and moving into Germany. Demands were made and sent to Prague. The tension began to mount.

By 20 May 1939 the Czechs were convinced Hitler was about to send the boys in armed to the teeth to force the issue. As a pre-emptive measure, the Czechs decided to mobilise.

To say this annoyed Hitler was an understatement. He was incandescent with rage. His mood was made even worse with France and Britain tapping him on the shoulder warning him that if anything kicked off with Czechoslovakia it would start another European war.

The irony of it all was that Hitler hadn't actually intended to invade Czechoslovakia – well not yet anyhow. The plans for 'Case Green' the codename for the invasion were almost finalised, but now there would have to be a delay. Europe was far too alert and it was too much of a risk. Instead on 23 May the German Foreign Office informed Prague that Germany had 'no aggressive intentions' when it came to their country.

After moping about in a bit of a sulk for a few days, Hitler resolved to wipe Czechoslovakia off of the face of the planet. Quickly. He instructed his army generals to ensure that 'Case Green' be carried out by 1 October 1938 at the very latest.

The thing is, the Army Generals were getting a little bit fed up with Hitler's ranting and raging. They didn't like his aggressive attitude towards the rest of Europe, and they were convinced his actions would take them to an all-out war with France, Britain and probably Russia. A war Germany would not (in their opinion) win. This opposition was led by chief of the Army of the General Staff, General Ludwig Beck who called on his fellow officers to unite and stand up against Hitler and his Nazi thugs. If they all resigned the aggression must surely falter – there would be no one to lead the armies. Unfortunately despite much nodding of heads and muttering of agreement amongst the Army top brass, there was no action. The rest of the officer class were either too scared or too comfortable in their positions to go against Hitler. Dismayed, Beck resigned on 18 August.

The summer of 1938 also saw some political movement on the international situation too. The British Prime Minister was recorded as saying that he thought the Czech government should grant self-determination to the country's minorities, even if that meant them leaving the country. Intrigued at this take on the situation, the German Foreign Office did a little more digging and discovered that Chamberlain was happy enough for the Sudetenland area of Czechoslovakia to be handed to Germany as long as it was carried out after a legal and fair referendum and not by force. Russia also sent out sound bites that seemed to suggest she too was not keen on getting involved in the whole situation. It seemed to Ribbentrop and to Hitler that if they decided to act against the Czechs the consequences would be minimal.

Happy days.

Throughout the summer the German High Command busied themselves with the final preparations of 'Case Green' and on 12 September Hitler lit the touch paper with an angry speech in Nuremberg aimed squarely at the Czechs. He was out for blood, and so were the Sudetens. Whipped to a frenzy by Hitler's rhetoric they went on a two-day rampage which the Czech government only managed to stop after sending the troops in and proclaiming martial law.

The French were getting very nervous as they had obligations to protect the Czechs in the case of invasion. In desperation, the French asked Chamberlain to reach out to Hitler to see if he can diffuse the situation. The next day Chamberlain, who had never stepped foot on a plane before in his life, flew seven hours to the Berchtesgaden to speak face to face with Hitler in an effort to thrash out a deal. Hitler asked him straight – would Britain agree to the German annexation of the Sudetenland? In typical political fashion, Chamberlain refused to answer the question straight, preferring instead to insist he discussed it with his French friends. It was getting very close to a full on crisis. French forces had partially mobilised and moved up to the Franco/German border and Prague remained defiant. A final attempt at sorting this mess out in a diplomatic way was hastily organised when the leaders of Germany, Italy, France and Britain converged on Munich to thrash out a solution.

At Munich it was agreed that Germany should take the Sudetenland in return for a vague promise to respect the security of the rest of Czechoslovakia. The decision was made without the Czechs – they were not even invited to the conference. The people of Czechoslovakia had been betrayed.

The Sudetenland not only housed millions of Germans, it also contained over 60% of Czech coal production, 70% of her iron and steel production and 70% of her electric power generators. Not only had France and Britain deserted the Czechs, they had basically encouraged Hitler to go ahead and fill his boots. Hitler had got what he wanted, and so had Chamberlain. He returned to Britain a hero for averting war, proclaiming in triumph, 'I believe it is peace in our time.'

He would be sadly mistaken.

At ten minutes to one in the afternoon of 30 September 1938 Czechoslovakia surrendered. Right to the end Britain and France were in the Czech's faces making sure there was no last minute revolt against the terms of the surrender

The Czechs were helpless and hapless, and the vultures were circling – Poland and Hungary were keen to get a slice of the Czech action – and both helped themselves to thousands of square miles of territory. To rub salt into the wounds, Berlin forced the Czechs to install a pro-German government with a heavy Nazi representation.

Despite all of this though, Hitler was not totally satisfied. In his mind Munich was only a partial solution and a few days later he got busy on plans for finishing the job.

His plan was simple. Start a campaign of propaganda and subversion so intense as to threaten the break-up of the entire country of Czechoslovakia from within – then, under the pretext of 'restoring order', march his armies in and take control.

On March 14 1939 the German army was poised and ready to kick down the door to Czechoslovakia. In a last ditch attempt to save his country from destruction, Czech President Dr Emil Hácha went to Berlin to meet with Hitler and his government. The Germans hounded Hácha, literally chasing him around the table trying to push pens and documents in his hand to make him sign and hand over his country. They threatened to bomb Prague if he didn't sign immediately. Hácha actually collapsed under the strain and after he was revived by German medical staff he finally signed the document that placed his country and its entire population under the control of the Fűhrer.

At dawn on 15 March 1939 German troops crossed into Moravia and Bohemia and by the evening Hitler was sipping cocktails in Hradschin Castle in Prague. His revenge was complete.

Czechoslovakia was no more.

Kristallnacht

The Nazis didn't like Jews. They made that perfectly clear right from the outset and as soon as they came to power the Jewish community was the victims of continued oppression and violence. In those early days such attacks were not part of any coordinated centralised plan to destroy them as a race, that kind of organisation never actually appeared until 1940 and the 'Final Solution'. These first waves of attacks were localised and were often led by members of the SA or SS and meant to just terrorise and scare, and if there were ill-gotten gains to be had, then the SA or SS chaps involved were more than happy to trouser whatever loot they could.

On 1 April 1933 Hitler announced an official boycott of Jewish businesses. This was not entirely down to Hitler bowing to pressure from some of the more extreme members of his party, he was also responding to calls from the global Jewish community to boycott German-made goods in a show of solidarity for their German Jewish colleagues. The Nazi boycott was not a success, despite members of the SA standing outside Jewish run shops in an effort to intimidate shoppers, many members of the public thought the boycott was ridiculous and resented the fact they were being told to alter their shopping habits.

Regardless of public apathy, Hitler pressed ahead with his idea of ridding Germany of Jewish influence. In April 1933 the 'Aryan Clause' was introduced. It decreed that only individuals of Aryan decent, i.e. without Jewish parents or Grandparents, could work in the public sector and education. In June this law was extended to stipulate that even marriage to a non-Aryan individual would be enough to warrant exclusion from working in these areas. Initially Jewish holders of the Iron Cross and those who had served in the First World War were exempt, although this didn't last long. Very quickly 'enthusiastic' local Nazis were using the Aryan Clause as an excuse to kick out any Jew from any job they liked – including doctors and lawyers.

Slowly but surely Jewish business was destroyed. In the five years between 1933 and 1938 the number of Jewish businesses registered in Germany declined by 75%. Thousands of children of Jewish decent were also banished from schools – those that were allowed to attend schools were continuously bullied by the other children and their teachers. Then, in 1935, the Nuremberg Laws took the whole 'give-the-Jews-a-bit-of-kicking' attitude of Germany to the next level.

The Nuremberg Laws classified every citizen of Germany. Those with four German grandparents were deemed to be 'German' or 'Aryan' whereas those with three or four Jewish grandparents were officially classified as 'Jewish'. It was now illegal for any classified Jew to marry or cavort with any proper German. It was also made illegal for any Jew to employ a German woman who was under the age of forty-five, just in case any relationship between the two blossomed. The Nazis were doing everything they could to ensure the pure Aryan bloodstock was not tainted and polluted by any Jewish DNA.

As the years went on and each gamble the Reich took paid off (Anshcluss, Czechoslovakia etc.), the Nazis got bolder and brasher with their treatment of the Jews. By 1938 they didn't really give much attention to what the international community would do to try and stop them, the propaganda machine was in full swing and the violence was ratcheted up even more. Most of the Jewish influence in German business had been eradicated and the economy was doing alright thank you very much. Also, the Nazi top brass knew very well that war was on the horizon. They wanted to prepare the German public and get them re-conditioned to think that the Jews 'stabbed them in the back' in the last war. They were the enemy within.

Jewish doctors, dentists, vets and chemists were all banned from practicing. All Jewish people were forced to register their assets and on 17 August a new law was passed that forced all Jewish people to have a Jewish name and if they didn't have one they had to add either 'Israel' or 'Sara' to their name by 1 January 1939. This would make every Jew instantly recognisable and would only exacerbate their already significant separation from the rest of society.

Also in August, all permits for foreigners, including all German born Jews of foreign descent, were cancelled and had to be renewed. On 28 October 1938, on Hitler's direct orders, more than 12,000 Polish born Jews were ordered to leave their homes immediately – they were allowed just one single suitcase as they were crowded onto trains and shipped out to the Polish border. The problem was, when they reached the border and tried to get into Poland, Polish border guards refused them entry and sent them back. This situation lasted for days – thousands of Jews were quite literally left out in the cold. They had no food or shelter and the weather was miserable. Eventually four thousands of them were allowed in, the rest were simply made homeless at the frontier. If they tried to get back into Germany they were simply shot by the Gestapo.

Among those expelled were Sendel and Riva Grynszpan, Polish Jews who had settled in Hanover in 1911. Their seventeen-year-old son, Herschel, was living in Paris and he received a postcard on 3 November from his parents asking him to send them some money to help buy supplies. Four days later he purchased a pistol and some bullets and wandered into the German embassy in Paris and requested to see an official. He was taken to see Ernst von Rath, once in his office he fired off five shots into the diplomat. Grynszpan made no attempt to escape and confessed to French police immediately.

Ernst von Rath died of his wounds a few days later on 9 November. Ironically he wasn't a staunch Nazi, he actually had been quite vocal (as far as he was allowed to be) in his opinion about the harsh treatment of the Jews under the

Nazi regime, to such an extent he was being investigated by the Gestapo. On that same day Hitler and his cronies were having a bit of a celebratory bash commemorating the 1923 Munich Putsch, when he was told of von Rath's death Hitler immediately issued instructions for a huge, coordinated attack on German Jews. The murder, in his eyes, was a cold and calculated attack on the Reich by world Jewry and it couldn't go unpunished. Messages were sent out to Nazi Party regional offices to take swift and violent action against all Jews – especially their synagogues. Simultaneously messages were sent to Police commanders to make them aware of what was about to go down, and ordering them not to interfere.

Very quickly these instructions were received across the country. Thousands of SA and SS men flooded into the streets, many drunk after celebrating the Munich anniversary, and headed for the nearest synagogue. It wasn't long before practically every synagogue in the country was up in flames. When the fire services were called, many arrived in good time but actually sprayed their water on neighbouring buildings that were owned by Germans, to make sure they didn't catch fire too.

Kristallnacht – or the night of the broken glass – had officially started.

Synagogues were not the only target; storm troopers also had any Jewish shop in their sights. Windows and doors were smashed in and displays broken up, and any items that took their fancy were stolen, leaving the pavements covered in thousands of shards of broken glass, hence the name given to this particular episode in Nazi history.

Jewish homes were also targeted – thousands of Jews were woken up in the middle of the night by Gestapo, SA or SS troops armed with axes, guns, daggers and sticks, breaking into their house. Books, radios, cameras, jewellery, valuables and furniture were taken and many inhabitants were beaten up. There were even instances of Jewish gravestones being smashed to pieces.

In many ways Kristallnacht contained strong echoes of the scenes that occurred in Germany in 1933, however this time the violence was more extreme, more deliberate and more organised. Another factor was the way thousands of young kids and teenagers were actively involved in the violence, having been almost brainwashed into seeing Jews as criminals and enemies of the state both at schools and in organisations such as the Hitler Youth. These youngsters followed the storm troopers about, often diving into properties shortly after the main beatings had been dished out, to see what trouble they could cause.

As dawn broke the next morning, Hitler and Goebbels conferred and agreed to put a halt to the riots, although in some regions the violence and antagonisation continued. No one really knows how many deaths occurred during Kristallnacht. Official figures suggest ninety-one deaths, but many more probably died of wounds or committed suicide in the days afterwards. As well as these deaths, another 30,000 Jewish men were arrested and sent off to concentration camps where they were subjected to torturous conditions. In the Dachau camp many men were forced to stand to attention in the November winter for hours without adequate clothing. Anyone who moved was subsequently beaten by the SS guards.

The reaction to Kristallnacht by ordinary Germans was mixed. Many were shocked and stunned by the level of aggression and violence – although most were not shocked or stunned enough to offer any help to any Jewish family in need. The reaction from the Nazi top brass however, was single minded. On 12 November they all agreed to issue a string of decrees aimed at further restricting the rights of any Jew that had the temerity to stay in Germany after all that had happened. Using the murder of vom Rath as an excuse, Jews were banned from certain restaurants and hotel chains, as well as many public spaces including popular streets and upmarket residential areas. Jews were also barred from attending university.

They also announced that, from January 1939, all tax concessions were to be removed and a special high rate of income tax would be reserved specially for Jews. Not that there were many left in work, especially after another law was announced covering the Exclusion of Jews from German Economic Life was passed which banned Jews from almost all walks of German working life.

Finally, the Jewish community was ordered to pay a fine of one billion reichmarks as payback for the murder of vom Rath. Any Jew that was earning a wage had to hand over

20% of their assets by August 1939, and they had to clear up the mess left over from Kristallnacht at their own expense, although all insurance payouts for the damage was immediately confiscated by the government.

In the eyes of the Nazis Kristallnacht had been a roaring success and they were one step closer to the racial paradise they craved.

An angry Fűhrer and the Pact of Steel

It didn't take long after the whole sordid Czech affair for Chamberlain to realise what had actually happened. In a speech on 17 March he asked the world a rhetorical question: 'Is this the last attack upon a small state or is it to be followed by others?' In all honesty he knew the answer, and in a thinly veiled threat to Herr Hitler continued his speech with an air of defiance: 'No greater mistake could be made than to suppose that this nation has so lost its fibre that I will not take part in resisting such a challenge if it ever were made.'

If that wasn't clear enough to those nasty Nazis, he followed this up on 31 March with an address to the House of Commons in which he stated: 'In the event of any action which clearly threatened Polish independence and which the Polish government considered it vital to resist with their national forces, His Majesty's government would feel themselves bound to lend the Polish government all support in their power. I may add that the French government has authorised me to make it plain that they take the same position…'

Finally, someone in Europe was beginning to stand up to Hitler, and he was less than impressed. In fact when he heard about the PM's speech he flew off the handle in a rage of epic proportions – he was so mad he had to cancel a live radio broadcast, he instead recorded it so it could be edited afterwards in case he said something too inflammatory. He had to keep his public persona as calm as possible, even if he was raging inside.

And rage he did... to anyone who would listen. On 3 April he authorised Case White – the invasion of Poland – and told his Army big-wigs to get busy with preparations for the offensive. Meanwhile Europe once more descended into a flurry of handshakes, chess moves and finger pointing. Poland was in no fit state to resist any kind of military action from Germany. She was surrounded on three sides by enemy territory; she had no air force to speak of and a poorly trained and equipped army. Smelling blood, Mussolini sent some of his troops into Albania which scared the living daylights out of a number of small countries in the area. To counter this, Britain put a friendly arm around the shoulders of Greece and Romania and promised to protect their interests if they got dragged into the fight.

In response, and despite Hitler having a low opinion of the Italian military machine, Germany offered to join Italy in a military alliance – something which Mussolini jumped at and on 6 May 1939 agreed to all of the German conditions of the partnership. This 'Pact of Steel' was formally ratified in a glamorous signing ceremony in Berlin on 22 May.

Slowly but surely two distinct sides were beginning to form.

The day after the signing of the 'Pact of Steel' Hitler met with his military top brass again and explained to them the problem he needed to solve; the problem of Lebensraum or living space. In order for Germany to be self-sufficient he needed more space on which to grow crops and produce raw materials. So far they hadn't done so badly, Austria and Czechoslovakia had been brought under the wing of the Reich in relatively quick succession, but it wasn't enough and the next targets were unlikely to be so amenable to a union with Germany. There was no other alternative – Germany had to expand her empire in the east and that would mean war. Poland was first on his hit list in the east and if the west got involved then they would get a pasting too. Belgium and Holland first, then France. That would give them a decent base from which to attack Britain from the air and the sea.

The only problem with this plan was that everyone in the room, including the big man himself, knew deep down that despite all of the re-armament and recruiting that had gone on over the last few years to build up the Germany armed forces, they would never be strong enough to take on Poland, France, Britain and Russia all at once. If they were to be successful they had to prepare a lightning fast campaign that would knock out their targets before they had time to react and if possible they had to keep Russia out of it all together.

Best Friends Forever (sort of): Germany and Russia

As early as May 1939, Hitler had come to realise that if his plan to take Poland and other eastern European territories was to be successful he had to somehow or other negate the threat of Mother Russia. With Poland specifically, a laissez faire attitude from Stalin was essential due to the long Russian border along the eastern flank of Poland.

However, throughout mid-1939 it was the France and Britain that were in the box seat when it came to doing a deal with the Russians. In July that year the three countries agreed to meet to figure out a joint plan on how to deal with the potential threat of Hitler's Germany. However certain French and British dignitaries were skeptical of what Russia would actual bring to this party and were also at odds with each other as to what the terms of such an agreement between the three countries should look like. As such they were slow to send out a delegation to Moscow and when they did so they literally took a slow boat – a passenger liner that would take the best part of a week to arrive – the Allied group wouldn't get into Leningrad until mid-August.

Ever the opportunist, and a truster of no-one, Stalin kept his options open throughout the negotiations with France and Britain and secretly opened up discussions with the Nazis too. Hitler closely watched the situation unfold and saw that he had a window of opportunity to gazump the dawdling British and French group and get in first with his own deal with Stalin. Germany upped the pressure on Russia and sent off a number of telegrams to Stalin's office asking for an opportunity to sign peaceful pact between the two countries. They knew that deep down Stalin was a little wary of the Western capitalists and didn't entirely trust them. On August 19 Hitler received an answer from Stalin – he had seen a copy of the proposed non-aggression pact and was willing to see Ribbentrop on 26 or 27 August.

For Hitler this was close, but no cigar. He had a small window of opportunity here and needed to get the Russian deal done and dusted fast. Not only did he want to beat the French and British to the signature of Stalin, he had also just mobilised the thick end of a quarter of a million men in preparation for an invasion of Poland and didn't want them hanging around for nothing. He wanted to get on the road to Poland by 1 September so as to be enjoying a large chunk of Polish salami in Warsaw before the autumn rains set in. Time was of the essence.

In light of this, Hitler swallowed an awful lot of pride (bearing in mind what he had done to the local communists in Germany over the last few years) and practically begged Stalin to receive his foreign minister as soon as possible. After a nervous twenty-four hours which saw a very twitchy Führer get very distressed, Stalin sent his reply to Germany. By that time, talks between France, Russia and Britain had broken down, so Stalin agreed to meet with von Ribbentrop on 23 August in Moscow.

For Hitler, it was game on.

Von Ribbentrop got on a plane almost immediately and was in Moscow before you could say 'a bowl of cold soup and large vodka please, waiter'.

In the small hours of 23/24 August 1939 both Russia and Germany signed a ten-year non-aggression pact. By signing up, not only did each nation pinky-promise not to attack each other, but if one of them was set upon by another nation, the other party would remain neutral and not get involved, unless they felt compelled to support each other in the fight.

Those were the public parts of the treaty, there were also some not-so-public bits that were also agreed to; namely the division of Poland, Romania, Lithuania, Latvia, Finland and Estonia into Russian and German 'spheres of influence'. Under this secret squirrel part of the agreement it was agreed that Russia was to have Finland, Latvia and Estonia, the eastern part of Poland and the best part of Lithuania. The Nazis could have the rest.

On 24 August the Russian media went to press with stories of the new agreement. The story was met with shock and surprise from most parts of the globe, especially in the west who had no idea that Germany had been whispering in the ear of Russia for the last few months. The news was even a bit of a shock to Nazi allies such as Italy and Japan – the Nazi ambassadors to those countries had a busy time of it attempting to justify why they had suddenly decided to hold hands with their sworn enemy.

No sooner had the ink dried on those famous bits of paper, the French and British negotiation team urgently requested a meeting with the Russians to try and understand what was going on. They were told in no uncertain terms that 'in view of the changed political situation, no useful purpose can be served in continuing the conversation.'

Back home in Germany, convinced that now that Russia had swapped sides, Britain and France would not follow through with their promise to protect Poland; Hitler was in a good mood. A very good mood. In fact, he was in such a good mood he brought forward the invasion of Poland.

Case White would kick off on Saturday, 26 August 1939 at 04:30.

War

Everything was set. The generals had primed their men and they were ready to explode into Poland on the agreed date of 26 August. However, a couple of spanners (one of British origin and another of Italian design) were thrown into the works on 25 August which caused a few consternations in the Hitler household.

It was less than twenty-four hours before the 'go' button was due to be pressed, and Hitler was meeting with the British ambassador to Germany. During their meeting Hitler was keen to impress on the ambassador that he had no gripes with Britain and he was willing to do a deal that would guarantee the continuation of the British Empire in all circumstances. He even promised to come to the aid of Britain if she needed help to beat up any baddies.

Hitler had offered Britain a way out of the war, with guarantees that the Empire would stay as-is, and it all sounded fabulous... but it had one tiny little caveat. All of this goodwill and generosity from the German Reich would only come into effect AFTER Hitler had sorted out his Polish problem. The British ambassador nodded and made all the right noises during the meeting, and promised to take the matter up with London at once. Hitler was quietly confident that Chamberlain would accept the offer and take a seat at the back of the room, far away from the action.

His confidence would prove unfounded.

London replied by signing a formal Anglo-Polish treaty in which they promised Poland that if anyone started picking on them, they would come to their aid and give the bullies a bit of a British beating. Hitler's attempt to buy off Great Britain had failed.

The Fűhrer's mood was not helped much by news later that day that Mussolini had decided that the prospect of full-on war had come a few years too soon for his army, and if Hitler went ahead with the invasion of Poland, Italy would sit this particular dance out.

Needless to say Il Duce was not the most popular chap in the chancellery that evening.

In amongst all of the swearing, a decision had to be made. The German army was hours away from marching into Poland, should they just continue, or should Hitler call them back to give him time to clear his head and gather his thoughts based on the news he had received that evening. Eventually after much pacing about, he made the call:

All troop movements were to be stopped. The proposed invasion was called off. It was easier said than done and in a few places members of the German army did get across the border and started shooting up a few Poles, but they were quickly recalled and the Polish government didn't suspect what they had just missed out on.

On 31 August after a few days of frantic political feather rustling and desperate attempts at placation, Adolf Hitler issued his final order on the subject: the attack of Poland was to be carried out on 1 September at 4.45am

The war was back on.

He didn't really know how Britain and France would react. Would they honour their promise to Poland and meet him head on or would they turn a blind eye and let him get on with it as they did with the Czechs? As a million and a half German soldiers hot-footed it towards the Polish border intent on wreaking havoc – it was almost time to find out.

In an effort to make it seem that the Poles started it, a few groups of SS men dressed up in Polish uniform and faked Polish attacks on German radio stations and other buildings. They even dressed up concentration camp inmates in SS uniforms and shot them to make it look that little bit more realistic. At daybreak, the military might of Germany poured into Poland and headed straight for Warsaw.

Back home in Berlin there was general apathy to the historical news that greeted them when they woke up later that morning. There were no cheering crowds like 1914, the streets were not full of marching soldiers being bombarded with flowers and flags and keepsakes by young German lovelies. There was nothing. Even his speech in the Reichstag which attempted to justify his decision to go to war was met with only muted applause.

It didn't matter though, because their Fűhrer had made the decision for them. Germany was at war with Poland and two days later, on 3 September, Britain and France climbed through the ropes and entered the ring too.

The Second World War had officially started.

Blitzkrieg and initial victories

Poland had been an 'issue' for Germany since 1919. In the Treaty of Versailles, Poland was rebuilt and given some extra land – dubbed the Polish Corridor – that not only used to be part of the German Empire but also left the region of East Prussia detached from the rest of Germany. Then there was the city of Danzig that was governed by the League of Nations – despite a large German population. Taking this into consideration, it was perhaps no wonder that relationships between Germany and Poland were frosty at best throughout the twenties and thirties.

When the German army crossed the Polish border in the small hours of 1 September 1939 all of this built-up frustration was channeled into a new kind of warfare. A warfare more intense, more violent and more destructive than anyone had witnessed in history.

Blitzkrieg.

As hundreds of fighter planes and bombers roared across Polish skies destroying strategic targets to a tight schedule, the tanks, the artillery and other motorised armour smashed their way through the country, advancing up to forty miles a day. Nothing could stop them. On top of that a million and a half men wearing the Nazi eagle followed tightly behind connected with all the other elements of the advance via a huge network of super advanced communication systems. It was the largest coordinated strike ever and unlike any major offensive in the history of major offensives.

The Poles battled bravely but they were woefully under prepared for the whirlwind. Within forty-eight hours the Polish air force ceased to exist and a week later the Polish infantry followed the same fate.

Two days later France and Britain declared war on Germany, in defence of Poland. On 7 September ten French infantry divisions pushed nervously five miles into German Saarland – that was about as much support as the Poles got from their two western Allies. They had been promised the making of a second front in the West by the 17 September, but that didn't materialise. Instead, on that day the Poles got another surprise present; the Russians invaded from the east. Within a matter of days Stalin had expanded the territory of Mother Russia by a handy 77,000 square miles and 11,000,000 people, including about a million Jews. Meanwhile France and Britain did nothing. France was simply not ready for war, and flatly refused to assault the Siegfried Line. Even when asked to drop a few bombs on Berlin both the French and Britain quickly changed the subject. They didn't want the Luftwaffe to retaliate with bombing raids against their own cities.

In a matter of weeks Poland had gone the way of Austria and Czechoslovakia – it had disappeared. On 5 October Hitler made a triumphant entry into what was left of Warsaw

Hitler may have won the battle against Poland, but the real victors were the Russians. Stalin had got his hands on half of Poland and had the Baltic States in a stranglehold. In doing so he had also blocked Hitler from getting access to the vast Ukrainian wheat fields and Romanian oil – both were strategic assets he craved in an effort to make Germany self-sufficient. Even the Polish oil fields were now in Russian hands.

Meanwhile back in Germany, all of the time, money and effort Hitler had poured into military expansion was beginning to take its toll on civilian life. To pay for all of the guns Hitler had almost bankrupt his country and almost all manufacturing was given over to the military cause. As a consequence Germany's infrastructure was crumbling before their eyes and coal supply for domestic use was intermittent at best. The Gestapo was reporting widespread unrest from the population that was already getting fed up with their Führer's obsession with the military.

And the thing was, the German military machine still wasn't properly ready for a full on European war. The Polish campaign, for all its devastating speed and lightening strikes by air and ground, showed that the German army was vitally short of guns and vehicles of all sizes and descriptions. When Hitler expressed his wish to commence proceedings in the west his army generals strongly opposed. They wanted time to strengthen; there was also the question of the weather which had turned for the worse. Despite Hitler becoming furious at the prospect of a delay, they managed to convince him to postpone until the spring.

When Blitzkrieg did arrive in the west in early 1940, it wasn't in France as one would have expected. It was in Scandinavia.

Soon after Polish dust had settled, Stalin invaded Finland. France and Britain set about organising a small expeditionary force to help out the Finns, but they could only get there if they crossed through Sweden and Norway. Sweden was a vital source of iron ore for Germany, in the summer months this could be transported via the Baltic which was out of reach of the Allies, however in the winter the Baltic route froze over and the iron ore had to be shipped by rail to Norway and then shipped down the Norwegian coast to Germany. In Hitler's eyes, if the Allies were allowed to cross the continent en route to Finland they could also interfere with their iron ore supply – and that simply wouldn't do.

In the small hours of 9 April 1940 the Danish and Norwegian governments were handed an ultimatum which they were forced to accept immediately. Even as the documents were being read the German army were going through the final checks before they set off to smash Scandinavia. The Danes didn't have a hope, there was no way they could defend against the might of the panzers and before most Danish citizens had woken up that morning they had effectively surrendered to the Nazi machine.

In Norway, however, it was a bit different.

Despite all the key ports and coastal towns falling into German hands within hours of the initial advance, the King of Norway and his government refused to capitulate. The Nazis tried to talk the King into doing what they saw as 'the right thing' and handing his country over to Hitler – their tactics switched from flattery to intimidation and when neither of those worked they resorted to trying to wipe him off the planet. The King and his entourage were forced to flee into the forests. Meanwhile the British had regrouped and were having a go at kicking the Germans out of Narvik. However in early May, the French and British started making plans to get out of Norway as the feeling was that an attack on France was just days away – they left the Norwegians to continue the fight practically on their own.

10 May 1940 was an interesting day. In Britain, Neville Chamberlain was replaced as Prime Minister by Winston Churchill. On the same day Germany initiated the invasion of Belgium, the Netherlands and Luxembourg. In doing so they broke through the French line by pushing their mighty panzers directly through the Ardennes – something the Allies thought would never happen. Now, all of France was at Hitler's mercy.

On 22 June 1940 the French surrendered to Germany. The Armistice was signed in the very same railway carriage which witnessed the German capitulation in 1918.

It had taken just twenty-two years; Hitler now had his revenge. Not only that, but many countries, witnessing the might of the German Reich thought it in their interest to partner up with the Nazis and become Hitler's new best friend. In quick succession the likes of Hungary, Romania, Japan, Slovakia, Yugoslavia, and Croatia swore to the Nazis that they would jump in the ring on their side. In addition other neutral countries such as Portugal, Spain and Switzerland saw that it was advantageous to them to help out the Germans however they could.

By autumn 1940, Britain was isolated and Hitler had the whole of Europe at his mercy. Then, on 22 June 1941, Hitler attacked Russia. Operation Barbarossa would be the largest military operation ever launched, but it would also spell the beginning of the end of the Third Reich.

Genocide

To anyone who had taken any notice of what Hitler and his Nazi cronies and been screaming about since the early thirties, it was no surprise when the SS boys started to dish out severe beatings to the Jews of Europe. By the time the Germans had declared war on Russia in June 1941 and on the USA in December of the same year, the Nazi fantasies regarding world Jewry were on a whole new plain. In the mind of the Nazis, the Jews were responsible for the expansion of the war. Jews were intrinsically involved in both Bolshevism (USSR) and capitalism (USA) and the top men of both countries, Stalin and Roosevelt, were just tools in pawns in a game that international Jewry were playing in their attempt to take over the world.

It was a crazy idea and they were all delusional, but they held a gun to the head of most of Europe and at that particular time there was no one was brave enough to tap any of the leading Nazis on the shoulder and tell them to get back in their box.

To Hitler, Himmler and the rest of the Nazis, the Jews and the Slavs were untermenschen (subhumans) and in their eyes they had no right to live, apart from the 'lucky' ones chosen to work in the fields and mines as slaves for their Aryan 'masters'. The major eastern cities such as Warsaw,

Moscow and Leningrad were to be razed to the ground and the entire culture of the Russians, Poles, Czechs and the rest of the Slavs were to be completely destroyed.

In the early days of the war the Nazi ideal was to round up as many Jews as possible and put them in a special internment camp somewhere remote, somewhere out of the way so they couldn't 'infect' the rest of the Reich. The first step in this process was the setting up of ghettos, these were walled areas in cities and towns where all the Jews could be relocated prior to them being shipped off further east. The inaugural Polish ghetto was opened in October 1939 and many more followed in short order. The Warsaw ghetto was established in October 1940 and very soon afterwards around 380,000 people were crammed in to a small area of the Polish capital. Completely sealed off from the outside world those people that were imprisoned within their walls were susceptible to acute hardship, hunger and disease. Thousands died.

When the German soldiers first entered Russia they were treated as liberators by many locals who were fed up with living in and being terrorised by Stalin's regime. Indeed there were some people that thought if Hitler played his cards right he could have infiltrated the population and caused the collapse of Bolshevism from the inside. But he was consumed by an acute desire to destroy. In a memo sent to all senior officers in June 1941 they were told in no uncertain terms that 'This battle demands ruthless and energetic measures against Bolshevik agitators, guerrillas, saboteurs, Jews, and a complete elimination of any active or passive resistance'. And this was a message sent to the regular army – the instructions being sent out to the chaps of the SS was on a whole different level.

Hot on the heels of the invasion forces were special Einsatzgruppen (extermination groups) made up primarily of SS and police that had a very specific job: the murder of Jews, Romany, Communists and other perceived enemies of the state. The modus operandi of the Einsatzgruppen was simple, crude, but ultimately effective:

Step 1: round up the victims

Step 2: transport them to a pre-designated killing area

Step 3: shoot the lot of them

Massacres like this took place all over the eastern occupied territories, one of the nastiest actions was at Babi Yar ravine near Kiev where over 33,000 Jews were shot in September 1941. That's enough people murdered in one place in one day to fill a decent sized football stadium. Around the same time Himmler travelled to Minsk to visit Einsatzgruppe B and see them in action. An eye witness watched Himmler as his men shot one hundred Jews:

"As the firing started, Himmler became more and more nervous. At each volley, he looked down at the ground... The other witness was Obergruppenfuehrer von dem Bach-

Zelewski... Von dem Bach addressed Himmler: "Reichsfuehrer, those were only a hundred... Look at the eyes of the men in this commando, how deeply shaken they are. Those men are finished ["fertig"] for the rest of their lives. What kind of followers are we training here? Either neurotics or savages."

Arad, "Belzec, Sobibor, Treblinka", p. 8

After his visit to Minsk, Himmler was overcome by a sense of conscience. Well, sort of. He demanded a more 'humane' method of extermination be found. By November 1941 work had begun on the construction of an extermination facility at Belzec in Poland and more were being planned including a large crematorium at Auschwitz.

Racial genocide was just about to go industrial.

What the Nazis were planning had never been done before – to exterminate an entire race was an incredible undertaking and, leaving all emotion at the door, had the potential to be an enormous logistical nightmare. If they were to carry out this task and succeed in doing so they needed to have an efficient process and there were many questions still unanswered. In an effort to sort all this out, Heydrich chaired the Wanasee Conference on 20 January 1942.

At the conference, Heydrich addressed handpicked representatives from several government ministries and the

SS. He advised them that his calculations suggested that there were 11,000,000 Jews in Europe, half of which were residing in countries outside of the Reich. He spoke for an hour and then the group discussed the whole situation for another thirty minutes. The meeting was not designed to agree or disagree about whether to kill Jews or not, that decision had been taken a long time ago, the real reason was to talk through the practicalities of the process, and to make it clear that from now on the Final Solution to the Jewish question was a matter for the SS and the SS alone. No one present voiced any concerns. Heydrich was clear to go on his merry way.

In 1942 extermination camps were built at Treblinka, Sobibór, Chelmno, Majdanek and Belzec. Auschwitz, which was already set up as a work camp, enjoyed a huge new extension (Birkenau) which also held extermination and cremation facilities. It is almost impossible to get completely accurate numbers but it is estimated that these camps murdered anywhere between 2,700,000 and 3,000,000 Jews before the end of the war, with 1,000,000 dying at Auschwitz alone, with another 250,000 non-Jews killed there just for good measure. At Auschwitz, the killing method of choice was gas in the form of crystals that were poured into large rooms through special openings in the roof. Once in contact with the air the crystals vaporised and turned into a highly toxic gas that made short work of anyone breathing it in. It made the mass killings of Jews very simple indeed.

All in all it is estimated that around 5,000,000 Jews were killed during the Holocaust.

The turning of the tide: 1942-43

The war in Europe was all President Roosevelt's fault.

That was the essence of a speech given by a certain Adolf Hitler to the Reichstag on 11 December 1941. He declared brazenly that it was Roosevelt who had actually started the war. In fact he and his Jewish friends had been trying to sabotage peace in Europe since 1938. Their devious actions had forced the Nazis to go on the offensive purely as a form of self-defence.

He had obviously forgotten about the annexation of Austria, the taking of Czechoslovakia and the brutal invasion of Poland. Or perhaps these actions and the subsequent conquering of the majority of Western Europe were the legitimate reaction of a peaceful country. Yes, that's right, forget about the death squads, the murders, the concentration camps, the torture and the slave labour; the Germans were the real victims in all of this.

Delusional.com

But Hitler truly believed this. So did the rest of his Nazi mates. So much so, that on the same day he delivered this speech Germany declared war on the United States of America. Suddenly, the Third Reich was at war with three of the biggest superpowers on the planet.

It would surely only end in tears.

However, two-thirds of the way through 1942 Hitler was practically King of Europe. He also presided over a decent chunk of Africa to boot. Maps of the continent showed a Third Reich that stretched from the Arctic Ocean to Egypt and right across to Central Asia. On top of this, German U-boats dominated the Atlantic Ocean, sinking hundreds of thousands of tonnes of Allied shipping every month. Everything Hitler had touched thus far had turned to gold and he saw nothing in America to suggest any threat to his massive Reich.

Yet despite this, all was not rosy in the Nazi garden.

As a consequence of the huge amount of land now in Nazi hands, the flanks of the German army were simply enormous, and were largely held by weaker detachments made up of Hungarian or Romanian troops. All of these troops were inadequately equipped and often they were so remote that the supplies, artillery and armour they needed to function correctly frequently failed to appear.

Quite simply the Reich was being stretched too thin.

With the USA now in the fight, Hitler had to finish off the Russians as quickly as possible. As a consequence he urged his eastern armies to redouble their efforts and give the Communists a good hard kicking and put them out of their misery. He demanded, in a famous order given on 23 July 1942 that both Stalingrad and the Caucasus be attacked at the same time. It simply couldn't be done and his army generals knew it but if they tried to suggest anything they were moved out of office. In the end it was a decision that would signal the beginning of the end of the Third Reich.

The fighting in the east became Verdun-esque in its brutality and as they approached Stalingrad it was only going to get worse. There the Russians, for so long on the retreat, decided to stand and fight.

Meanwhile events in the south were about to take a turn for the worse too. By the end of October 1942 the British had finally got round to reinforcing its Egypt contingent and quickly launched a major offensive. Field Marshall Rommel was on his sick bed in Austria as all this was going on, and by the time he got back into the action it was as good as over. The British were too strong and his plea for more men, more guns and more planes fell on deaf ears back in Berlin. Within a matter of weeks the Afrika Korps had been pushed back over 700 miles.

1942 went from bad to worse in November when General Dwight D. Eisenhower led a large Anglo-American force into Morocco and Algeria, and started to advance quickly. Then, a few days later, back in the east, Russia went on the offensive. Big time.

By January 1943 what was left of the German Sixth Army was completely surrounded, cut off and quite literally on its knees. That mighty army strode into Russian territory just a few months earlier boasting 285,000 men; on 31 January

1943 only 91,000 were still breathing and they meekly surrendered to the Russians.

Things were not going according to plan for the Fűhrer, and it seemed his 'friends' were deserting him when he most needed them. Japan was ignoring repeated pleas to open up a second front with Russia and the Italians were getting increasingly nervous about the whole situation in southern Europe and north Africa. When the Allies invaded Sicily in the summer of 1943 the war suddenly became very, very real for the Italians and their nervousness rapidly descended into blind panic. Mussolini was kicked out of office, and arrested, and by September 1943 the Italians were sitting around the negotiation table talking about an Armistice.

Hitler reacted quickly to this Italian defection and moved in German troops to lock down the southern front, occupying the northern half of Italy in the process. He then turned his attention once again to the east, retribution was on his mind and with Operation Citadel he planned on crushing the Red Army with an immense show of armoured power, centred around the town of Kursk.

The Germans were defeated within two weeks.

To rub salt into the Nazi wounds, the Russians then went on an offensive of their own and pushed the German frontier right back into East Prussia, liberating many areas such as Ukraine, the Crimea and much of Poland and inflicting almost a million German casualties (killed/missing/wounded/prisoner) on their way. Such losses were slowly bringing the German army to its knees.

Meanwhile, the Allies were busy plotting the re-opening of the western front.

White roses and bomb plots: Germany starts to turn

Whilst Germany was enjoying a flourishing economy (on the surface at least) and a renewed sense of national pride with the growth of her armed forces no-one had a bad word to say about the Nazis. When Austria, Czechoslovakia and Poland were taken in as part of the Reich, most people rejoiced and backed Hitler. He was doing exactly as he had promised back in the thirties – to revive the German nation and get her back to her rightful place at the top table of world super-powers.

Everything was going very well thank you for asking.

But then things did start to go wrong. Defeat in Africa, followed by retreat and ultimate defeat in Russia, then the Luftwaffe went completely AWOL and allowed the RAF and USAF to dominate European skies. Costly defeats followed costly defeats and not even the great Dr Goebbels and his fantastic propaganda machine could bluff its way out of the hole Germany seemed to be digging for herself.

The dissenters started to grumble. Quietly. Nazi Germany was a police state after all and any perceived insolence was quickly squashed by the Gestapo. After the German invasion of Russia in 1941 a few Communist dissenters lifted their heads above the parapet but the Gestapo quickly had them in their sights and by early 1943 all the major Communist cells had been broken up, their ringleaders either executed or in concentration camps.

Another anti-establishment group was known as the White Rose Movement. Ironically this group was based out of Munich – the spiritual home of Nazism – and ran by a bunch of students from the city's university. It was only a small group of students and they kept it that way on purpose, they knew that the more people they had in their group the greater chance of them all being caught and that would not have been pretty. Between the summer of 1942 and early 1943 the White Rose Movement was relatively prolific in distributing anti-Nazi leaflets and they even embarked on a graffiti campaign throughout the city. The group were headed up by a brother and sister team of Hans and Sophie Scholl and the tone of their leaflets and messaging was very openly against the atrocities against the Jews as well as being against Hitler's overall leadership of Germany and they tried to rally the students to take a stand against the regime.

Hans and Sophie were caught red-handed distributing leaflets on 18 February 1943 by the Gestapo. They were subsequently tried and executed on 22 February.

The text of their final leaflet was smuggled out of Germany and handed over to the advancing Allies before the war ended. Millions of copies were printed and air-dropped all over the country.

Small civilian groups such as the White Rose Movement didn't really stand a chance of overthrowing the Nazi machine, however as the military situation became more and more desperate in 1943 and the prospect of an Allied invasion in the west was only a matter of time, a small group of anti-Nazis including some high ranking army officers, decided it was time to take matters into their own hands. During 1943 and early 1944 there were at least four attempts on Hitler's life from these army conspirators, they all failed, and as the war situation deteriorated Hitler became more and more of a recluse, rarely appearing in public and hardly ever meeting people he didn't know or trust intimately. Also, by the summer of 1944 the Gestapo were getting suspicious of one or two key personalities within the conspiracy group and were getting too close for comfort – they had to act quickly or forget the whole thing.

One of the leading figures in the conspiracy team was a young staff officer; Lieutenant Colonel Claus Schenk Graf von Stauffenberg. He had been badly wounded in North Africa where he lost his left eye, right forearm and a couple of fingers from his left hand. He was no Communist or raving lefty, but he was deeply opposed to what was going on with the Jews and Soviet prisoners and thought that by removing the top man, Germany would be in a better position to negotiate a tolerable peace settlement with the Allies.

After being promoted to Colonel towards the end of June 1944 and given decent access to Hitler directly, he was a good person to carry out the assassination attempt.

Von Stauffenberg was summoned to an operations meeting at Hitler's 'Wolf's Lair' in Rastenburg on 20 July 1944. To this meeting von Stauffenberg carried an English-made time bomb which, when he entered the room, had already been triggered and had around six minutes to run before it blew the place to pieces. Being late to the party meant that all the good seats next to Hitler had been taken, although he did manage to squeeze himself in so his was just a few feet from his Fűhrer. He put his briefcase, which carried the bomb, on the floor underneath the large table they were all standing round and pushed it under the table where it rested on the inside of one of the tables thick supporting legs – it was just a few feet its intended target.

Because von Stauffenberg didn't fancy getting blown up himself that day he managed to sneak out a few minutes before 'boom time' without anyone noticing. Shortly after he had left the room another officer present, Colonel Brandt, wanted to get a better look at the map and moved von Stauffenberg's briefcase out of his way to the other side of the supporting leg – further away from Hitler. It was a move that most certainly saved Hitler's life, but cost Brandt his.

At 12.42pm on 20 July 1944 the bomb went off, but had it done its job?

From where von Stauffenberg was (in front of a bunker a few hundred yards away) it looked conclusive. As he saw the debris and the bodies flying in the air after the explosion he was convinced Hitler was dead. Immediately he set off to initiate 'Operation Valkyrie' – the mobilisation of the German Reserve Army to form a coup.

However, Hitler wasn't dead. That table leg had saved his life and as soon as senior Reserve Army officers knew this they quickly turned on the conspirators. The plot failed.

In the aftermath of this failed coup around 7,000 people were arrested – not all of them were directly involved in the plot, but in true time-honoured Nazi fashion, the Gestapo took the opportunity to hand out beatings to other people that had been annoying them. 4,980 people were put to death, including of course von Stauffenberg who was executed by firing squad on 21 July 1944.

Liberation and disintegration: 1944-45

Hitler had an inkling that 1944 would be a key year for the Third Reich. In his New Year's Day speech to the German people he told them that over the next twelve months, 'this momentous war will approach its climax.' He knew the war was in the balance and in other speeches in the early part of the year warned all of Europe that a defeat to Germany would mean the end of the old Europe and a triumph for Bolshevism and world Jewry.

The year started in a mixed vein for Germany. American and British troops landed at Anzio in southern Italy in late January and threatened to push on quickly, however a swift mechanised counter-attack from the German panzers managed to put the Allies back in their place and stabilise that particular area. The same thing happened in the east with Russia threatening to push further into the Third Reich following on from their successes before Christmas. They made good and rapid progress, especially in the south where they reached the Moldavia border in early March and crossed into Romania in early April. However, overstretched supply lines meant this particular Russian offensive petered out.

It then all seemed to settled down a bit, until the month of June came knocking...

As bad months go, June 1944 has to be right up there as one of the all-time bad months for the Nazis. In the east the Allies successfully re-opened the western front with a huge seaborne landing on the beaches of Normandy, in the south Rome had fallen to the advancing Americans and in the east Russia launched an intense offensive that pushed German troops back rapidly.

From June until the end of the war the German army would be continually on the retreat in all theaters of the war. For Hitler and the Third Reich the writing was very much on the wall.

In France the Allies made short work of the much hyped Atlantic Wall after landing on the beaches of Normandy on D-Day. The German Army was caught sleeping – quite literally – and as their Fűhrer slept peacefully the Allied invasion force faced only sporadic opposition to their beach landings and quickly established a toe-hold on French soil. Once the Germans finally organised themselves they put up a decent defensive fight and the ensuing battle for Normandy became a bitter struggle for every cross roads, every hedgerow and every sunken lane. It took weeks for the breakout to happen and the costs to both sides were very heavy.

Paris was eventually liberated by Allied forces on 25 August 1944. Meanwhile, in the east the Russian army smashed through Poland towards the city of Lvov. In just ten days almost the whole of German held southern Poland was now in Russian hands. The Red Army also liberated the concentration camp at Maidanek where the outside world saw for the first time hard evidence regarding Jewish genocide. By late July, the Red Army – although they were exhausted and once again on the very edge of their supply lines – were knocking at the door of Warsaw.

The Warsaw population saw an opportunity for an uprising and attempted to liberate the city before the Russians did it. Bitter fighting for two months between Germans and Poles ensued ended with a Polish surrender on 1 October. In a brutal act of retribution the Germans then set about the Polish population in a big way – killing 225,000 people.

Towards the end of August the Russians flung themselves once again eastwards, this time towards Romania and South Ukraine. By early September the vast majority of Romania had been captured, including the vital Ploesti oil fields. Romania surrendered and with that opened the way up for Russian liberation of Hungary and Bulgaria.

There were pockets of strong German resistance to the Allied tidal wave, most notably at Arnhem, and there was even a decent offensive carried out in the Ardennes – the Battle of the Bulge – but it couldn't be maintained even though Hitler kept on pouring men and resources into the battle, despite his senior officers urging him to pull back. This was another flawed decision made by Hitler, who was increasingly reverting back to his old ways of huge gambles and distorted views of reality, but this time lady luck was deserting him. By throwing in so many men and guns into the Ardennes he had nothing to bolster the eastern front if and when Russian renewed their attack – which they duly did in January 1945. The same was true when the Allies in the west resumed their march on Germany in February 1945. The German Army fought their hearts out to protect their Fatherland, but in the end they found themselves facing hugely superior forces on all fronts – they had no chance.

It wasn't long before the Russians were on German soil. In barbaric acts of revenge for what the Germans had done in Russia over the last few years, the Red Army raped and murdered their way towards Berlin. Once at the gates of the capital, they were met by a defence force made up predominantly of old men and children who grabbed what guns and ammunition they could, barricaded the roads and waited for the soviet tanks to roll on in.

Meanwhile, the leadership of the Third Reich was in complete disarray. Hitler married his long time mistress Eva Braun on 29 April when the Red Army were just a few streets away from his bunker. They both committed suicide the following day. The day after that, in the same bunker, Goebbels poisoned his six children. Then he and his wife, Magda, killed themselves. After having a severe falling out with Göring which ended up with the Luftwaffe leader being kicked out of the party as a traitor, Hitler had amended his succession plans and once Hitler was gone Admiral Karl Dönitz took sole charge of what was left of the Third Reich.

On 2 May 1945 the Berlin detachment of the German Army surrendered – the hammer and sickle flag was quickly raised above the Reichstag building. Five days later, 7 May 1945, the German government, represented by General Alfred Jodl, surrendered unconditionally to the Allies in Rheims, France.

The Third Reich had been defeated.

The Third Reich on trial: Nuremberg

After the end of the war, the Third Reich almost immediately 'vanished'. Departments ceased to function practically overnight; the SS and Gestapo were conspicuous by their absence, as if thinking that they would just be forgotten about as everyone was busy cleaning up after the war. Nazi members of all rank and seniority got busy destroying documents, tearing up their membership papers and 'losing' their medals – many went into hiding and a good deal of them decided it was better to commit suicide than face their crimes.

As the Allies had liberated vast chunks of Europe and seen first-hand the genocide, the murders and the atrocities that had happened at the hands of the Nazis, they all quickly decided that when the time came those who were involved would get suitably punished. Such crimes could not and would not go un-answered.

Their answer was a series of trials, thirteen in all, which were carried out in the city of Nuremberg. Nothing like this had ever been done before, and trying to come up with laws and procedures that would work according to the laws of France, Britain, the USSR and the USA was not easy. Eventually the relevant laws were worked out and the London Charter of the International Military Tribunal was issued on 8 August 1945. In principal this Charter identified three categories of crimes for which the defendants would be answerable: crimes against peace, war crimes, and crimes against humanity.

Nuremberg wasn't chosen by accident as the venue for the trials, not only was the local Palace of Justice a nice large building that was relatively undamaged and could cope with the amount of people involved in the trial, it had also been the city where the Nazis had held their annual propaganda rallies – it had been a strong symbol of Nazism and it seemed fitting that the era of Nazism should formally be put to bed there too.

In the end there were twenty-four representatives of the Third Reich that were initially brought to trial at Nuremberg and the International Military Tribunal put together four indictments which were levelled at the defenders in various permutations:

1) Participation in a common plan or conspiracy for the accomplishment of crime against peace

2) Planning, initiating and waging wars of aggression and other crimes against peace

3) War crimes

4) Crimes against humanity

Perhaps the most well known of the defendants was Hermann Göring who was arrested shortly after the war trying to make away with large amounts of loot. He thought, as he was one of the senior Nazis, he would be able to negotiate his way out of his predicament, but he was wrong and was quickly arrested and put behind bars. During the Nuremberg trials he maintained that the actions of the Nazi Party members were as a result of their nationalism and love for Germany. He tried to dominate the rest of the defendants and get them to follow his lead – especially when he enjoyed early victories during cross examination – however he was soon separated from the rest of the group and his influence upon them began to wane. A summary of the men and their sentences follows:

Martin Bormann

Nazi Party Secretary. Not actually present at the trial and sentenced in his absence. Bormann was not charged with Indictment 2. Sentenced to death.

Karl Dönitz

Commander of Germany's U-boats and from 1943 led the entire German Navy. Announced as Hitler's successor on the death of the Führer. Dönitz was not charged with Indictment 4. Sentenced to ten years in prison.

Hans Frank

As well as being Hitler's personal lawyer, Frank was also the Governor-General of the occupied Polish territories where he oversaw the segregation of Polish Jews into ghettos. Captured by the Americans on 3 May 1945, he tried unsuccessfully to commit suicide before the trials started. Not charged with Indictment 2. Sentenced to death.

Wilhelm Frick

Minister of the Interior until 1943 and one of the most senior Nazis on trial. He was present at the Munich putsch in 1923 and once in government he was instrumental in formulating the racial policy of the Nazi Party including the Enabling Act and the Nuremberg Laws that led many thousands of people to be locked up in concentration camps. Sentenced to death.

Hans Fritzsche

Made head of the wireless news service for the government in September 1932 before the Nazis came to power. Joined the NSDAP in 1933 and continued in his role of heading the radio department under Goebbels's Reich Ministry. He was responsible for controlling German news until May 1942 when Goebbels took over personal control. Not charged with Indictment 4. Acquitted.

Walter Funk

Hitler's Minister of Economics and head of the Reichsbank. Intrinsically involved in stealing millions of dollars' worth of Jewish property. Sentenced to life in prison. Released in May 1957 due to ill-health.

Hermann Göring

Established the Gestapo in 1933 and held several Ministerial positions. He was also commander of the Luftwaffe and the most senior Nazi on trial. In 1941 Hitler announced Göring as his successor in the event of his death, although this was revoked in the last weeks of the war. Sentenced to death but committed suicide just before his execution.

Rudolf Hess

Former Deputy Fűhrer, Hess was responsible for several departments including finance, foreign affairs, law, education and health. All legislation passed through his office and he organised many of the large Nazi rallies, often introducing Hitler onto the stage. In May 1941 Hess flew to Scotland to try and organise peace with Britain. He was captured and spent the rest of the war as a prisoner. Sentenced to life in prison.

Alfred Jodl

Senior army commander, gaining the position of Chief of the Operations Staff of the Armed Forces High Command. He signed the unconditional surrender document as a representative of the new German leader, Karl Dönitz. Sentenced to death.

Ernst Kaltenbrunner

The highest ranking member of the SS to stand trial. He succeeded Heydrich as the head of the SS Intelligence Services and as President of the International Criminal Police Commission (known today as Interpol). His rank and involvement within the SS meant he was directly involved with the mass murders of civilians via Einzatsgruppen units, as well as the running of the concentration camps and the general persecution of the Jews, Gypsies and other non-Aryan groups. He was not charged with Indictment 2. Sentenced to death.

Wilhelm Keitel

German Field Marshal who served as chief of the Supreme High Command of the German Armed Forces. In this role he was involved in the planning of all the army campaigns in both the east and the west, although he did advise against invading France and also opposed Operation Barbarossa.

Both times he was overruled by Hitler. Although not a Nazi, he was sentenced to death on the basis he signed many orders that requested enemy soldiers and political prisoners be executed.

Gustav Krupp

Senior Nazi industrialist after inheriting the Krupp industrial empire through marriage in 1906. During WWI the Krupp company dominated heavy arms and artillery manufacture in Germany. Despite being initially against National Socialism he was persuaded to help finance their 1933 election bid. Later, as the president of the German Chamber of Commerce he was responsible for eliminating as many Jewish workers from the economy as possible. Bedridden and senile at the time of the Nuremberg trial his initial charges were eventually dropped on medical grounds.

Robert Ley

A fanatical Nazi who commanded the German Labour Front. Absolutely complicit in the mistreatment of foreign slave labour workers and had been at numerous meetings of Hitler's inner circle where the regime's extermination programme was openly discussed. He committed suicide before sentencing began and therefore was never actually sentenced.

Konstantin Neurath

Served as German Foreign Minister from 1932 to 1938 until he was replaced by the more sympathetic von Ribbentrop. Also served as Protector of Bohemia and Moravia between 1939 and 1943 and it was his part in a harsh crackdown on local protesting students which resulting in over a thousand being sent to concentration camps which led him to be sentenced to fifteen years in prison. Although his rule was deemed too lenient for hard line Nazis and he was technically replaced by Heydrich. Released in November 1954 due to ill health.

Franz von Papen

Was Chancellor of Germany before Hitler came to power, thinking he could control Hitler he was one of the main people that persuaded President Hindenburg there was no risk in appointing Hitler as Chancellor. He left the government after the Night of the Long Knives but was given a new assignment as German ambassador to Austria. During the trial he was questioned over his role in Nazi aggression, especially with regards the Austria Anschluss. He was acquitted due to a lack of evidence.

Erich Raeder

Commander of the German Navy up to 1943 when he was effectively retired from active service by Hitler and given the role of Admiral Inspector of the German Navy. Not charged with Indictment 4. Sentenced to life in prison. Released in September 1955 due to ill health.

Joachim von Ribbentrop

Hitler's Minister of Foreign Affairs from 1938 to 1945. Actively involved in the invasions of Austria, Czechoslovakia and Poland, he was also closely involved in the 'Final Solution' urging diplomats in foreign countries under Reich control to speed up deportations. Sentenced to death.

Alfred Rosenburg

An influential Nazi who was one of the main developers of the Nazi idealology including Lebensraum, and the persecution of Jews. He was also assigned Reich Minister for the Occupied Eastern Territories and was directly involved in the mistreatment of millions of Slavs. Sentenced to death.

Fritz Sauckel

Senior figure in the Nazi slave labour programme, working under Göring and was instrumental in organising the forced labour of over four million foreign workers for the German war effort. Most of the labour was from Poland and Russia, and Sauckel and his gang didn't care much for the methods used in order to get the foreigners working for the Reich. Once in place, these workers were given starvation rations and no pay. For his troubles Sauckel was sentenced to death.

Hjalmar Schact

Pre-war Minister of Economics and president of the Reichsbank until he was dismissed in 1937. Not charged with Indictments 3 and 4 and eventually acquitted.

Baldur von Schirach

Leader of the Hitler Youth and also Gauleiter of Vienna. Not charged with Indictments 2 and 3. Found guilty of crimes against humanity for his role in the deportation of Vienna-based Jews to concentration camps in Poland. Sentenced to twenty years in prison.

Arthur Seyss-Inquart

Appointed Gauleiter of Holland in May 1940 where he introduced strict measures to combat resistance. He personally sanctioned the execution of several hundred political prisoners. He was also a rabid anti-Semite and worked hard to rid Holland of as many Jews as possible. Sentenced to death.

Albert Speer

Hitler's chief architect and Minister of Armaments and War Production. He was not charged with Indictments 1 and 2 but for his use of forced labour in his role of overseeing German weapons production, he was sentenced to twenty years in prison.

Julius Streicher

A prominent Nazi and the editor of the Nazi anti-Semitic newspaper Der Stűrmer. His publishing company also produced a number of anti-Semitic books for children. He was not a member of the military and did not actually plan the 'Final Solution', however his role in building up anti-Semitic feeling in Germany could not be ignored. He was not charged with Indictments 2 and 3 but still sentenced to death.

References, sources and further reading

Traditionally, the reference section of a history book is a neatly set out list of book titles, authors, publishers and publication dates.

Hopefully, as you have just read this book and perhaps even some of the other Layman's Guides you have realised that these are not like most traditional history books. These days the way we access information has changed beyond measure from how we did it just a few years ago. It won't be long before reference and source pages such as this one will just have one or two words: Google, Bing or perhaps another search engine of choice.

I have used the internet extensively in the research and composition of this Layman's Guide. There are a plethora of websites that cover the history of the Third Reich, some good, some not so good but most of them offer a great deal of information and images of all aspects of life under the Third Reich.

Wikipedia is an obvious resource and with the Third Reich there are many different Wikipedia pages that concentrate on all different facets of this era, although there is the usual caveat that goes along with all Wikipedia pages as sometimes they can mislead and misinform - I have tried to double check all information I have used from this site with other resources.

Many of the other 'usual web suspects' have also helped me with this book: The History Learning site (www.historylearningsite.co.uk) is a great resource and if you can navigate your way through the maze of First World War content which is understandably dominating the BBC's website at the moment, you can find some great stuff on the Third Reich there too: you can visit the website here: http://www.bbc.co.uk/history/worldwars/wwtwo/

As the Jews were one of the primary targets of the Nazi regime it is not surprising that there is a large amounts of Jewish content both on the web and in print that concerns itself with Nazi Germany and the Holocaust. The Jewish Virtual Library (www.jewishvirtuallibrary.org) and Yad Vashem (www.vadvashem.org) are two of the best ones out there, but there are many and any reader wanting to know what it was like to be a Jew living in Nazi Germany should browse these websites – they are eye opening, upsetting and humbling all at the same time.

Print wise I have used a wide range of books to help put this Layman's Guide together and readers who want to learn and read about the Third Reich in more detail are spoilt for choice: The defacto work on this subject in my opinion is the utterly brilliant The Rise and Fall of the Third Reich by William L. Shirer (Bison Books, 1987) – this book is fantastically illustrated and wonderfully written by a chap who was actually there – in my mind if you only read one book (other than this one) on Nazi Germany, read Shirer's.

Hot on his heels is Laurence Rees with his magnificent Nazis: A warning from history (BBC books, 1997) which also has a brilliant documentary, also put together by the BBC, which accompanies it beautifully.

The big hitters and Knights of the Realm are of course in attendance; Sir Max Hastings has produced another monster epic called All Hell Let Loose (Harper Press, 2011) and charts the rise and fall of the Third Reich indirectly through battles such as the early Blitzkrieg victories in the west, Operation Barbarossa in the east and the ultimate fall of the empire in 1945. A similar work is Sir Martin Gilbert's The Second World War (Phoenix, 2009). Yet even the mighty Hastings and Gilbert are beaten on 'epic-ness' by Richard J. Evans who wasn't satisfied with one monster publication – he has managed to push out three volumes on the Third Reich and if you have a few weeks spare, you could do worse than immersing yourself in The Coming of the Third Reich (Penguin, 2004), The Third Reich in Power (Penguin, 2006) and The Third Reich at War (Penguin, 2009).

Other single volume histories of the Third Reich can be found in Martyn Whittock's A Brief History of The Third Reich (Robinson, 2011) which is an excellent and very readable volume, and Richard Overy's The Third Reich: A Chronicle (Quercus, 2010) both of which would be excellent additions to anyone's library.

Some of the more somber works that I have read in preparation for this book include Nazi Germany and the Jews: 1933-45 by Saul Friedlander (Phoenix, 2014) and The White Rose: Munich 1942-1943 (Wesleyan, 2011) by Inge Scholl, the sister of Hans and Sophie Scholl, the founders of The White Rose movement who were both executed for their troubles.

Happy reading!

Final Thought

I really hope you liked this Layman's Guide. If you did, please take the time to leave a review on your local Amazon site. Nice reviews mean the world to me. If you didn't like it or think I can improve, then please drop me a line, you can contact me easily via my website www.scottaddington.com I welcome all feedback, the only way I will improve as a writer is to listen to the people who read my work!

Also, if you want to keep up to date with what I am doing, my thoughts on all things history, special offers and new books – why not sign up to my e-newsletter at www.scottaddington.com – every new subscriber gets a free gift!

Thanks once again!

Scott

About the Author

I am on a mission to write short, sharp history books that educate, entertain and inspire children, teenagers and adults who many not read 'traditional' history books very often.

My 'Layman's Guides' are perfect introductions to their given subject, I like to say that they are more like an informal chat over a cup of tea/coffee rather than a heavy and dull historical text. Currently I have five Layman's Guides published covering The First World War, The Second World War, Waterloo, D-Day and the Third Reich.

The Great War 100 is my attempt to tell the story of The First World War using nothing but infographics. This is a brand new way of telling history, it has never been done this way before and I hope that this style of communicating complex information opens up the subject to many new people - especially children.

Follow me on twitter @scott_addington or visit my blog at www.scottaddington.com

Want some free WW1 related stuff?

Visit http://www.scottaddington.com/free-stuff/

Printed in Great Britain
by Amazon